Like Lightning

COLORING BOOK

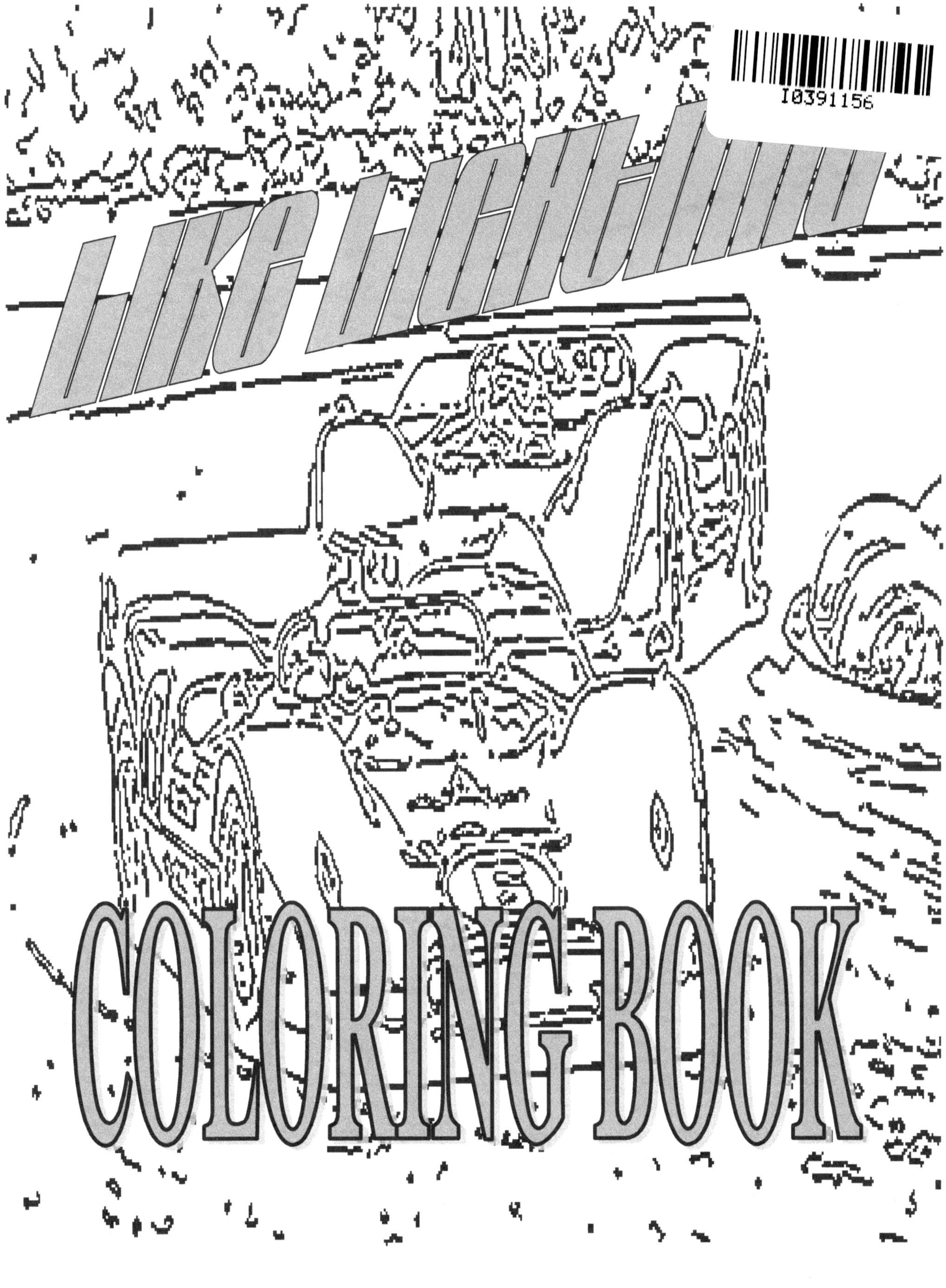

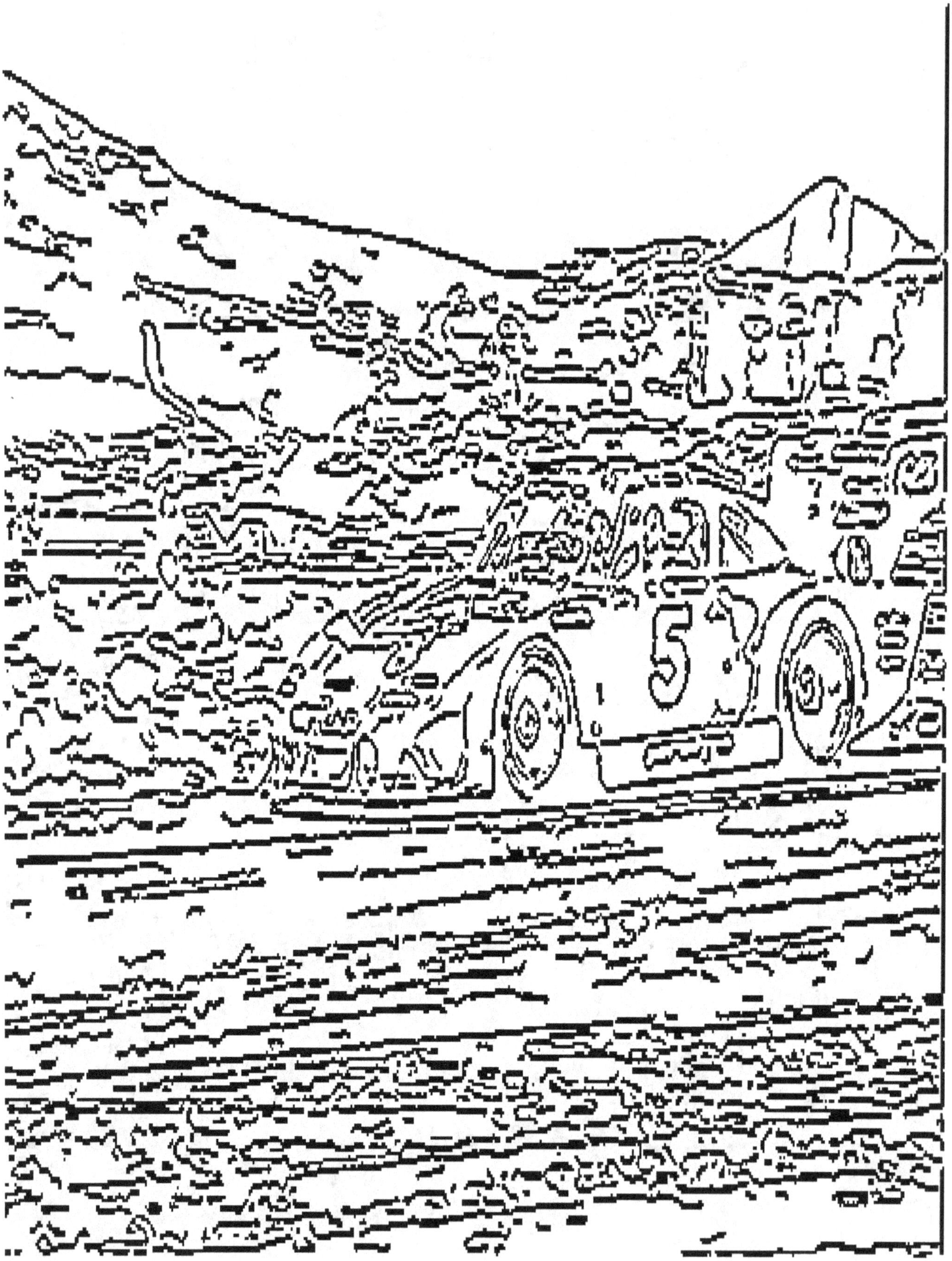
5

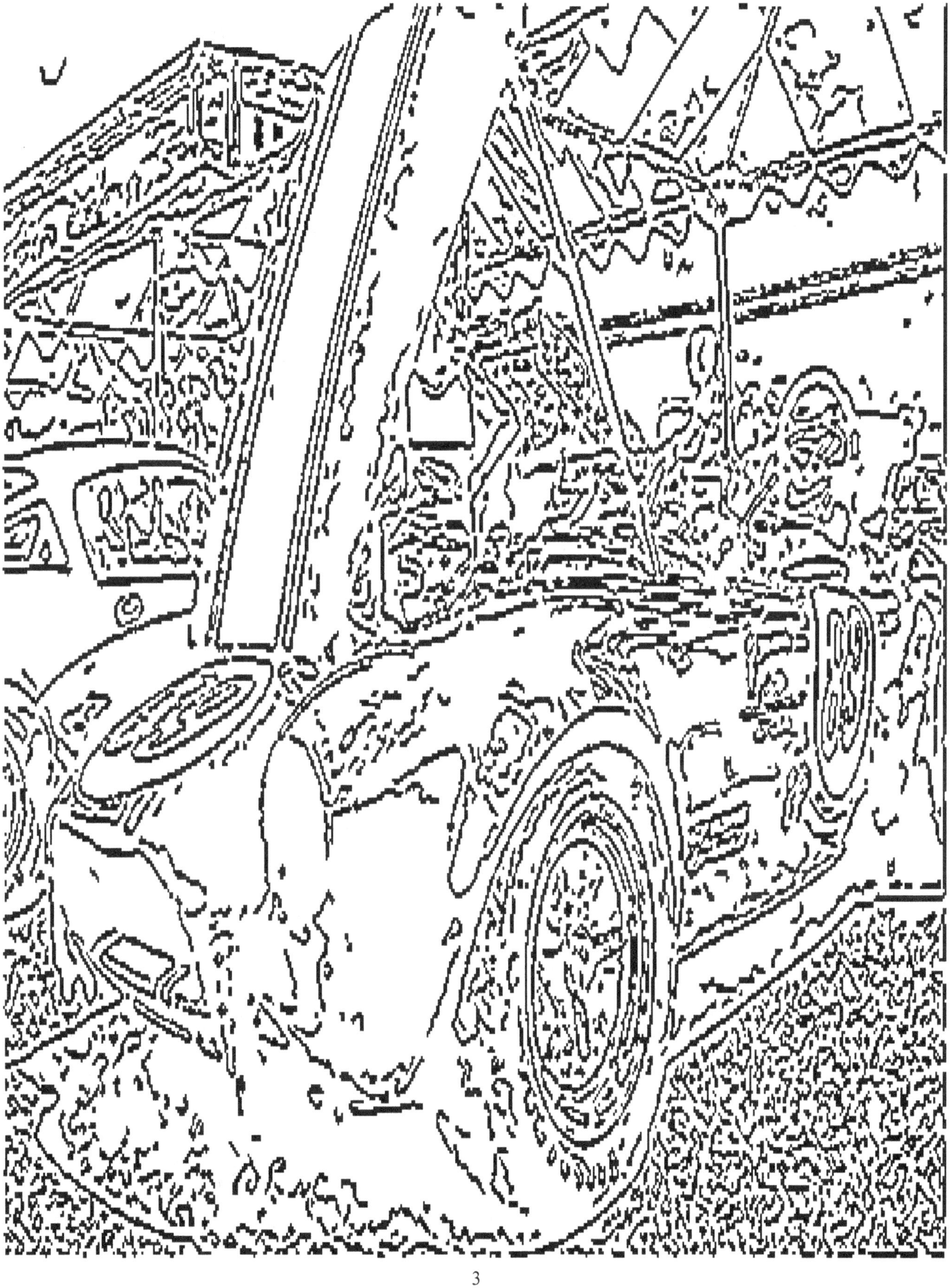

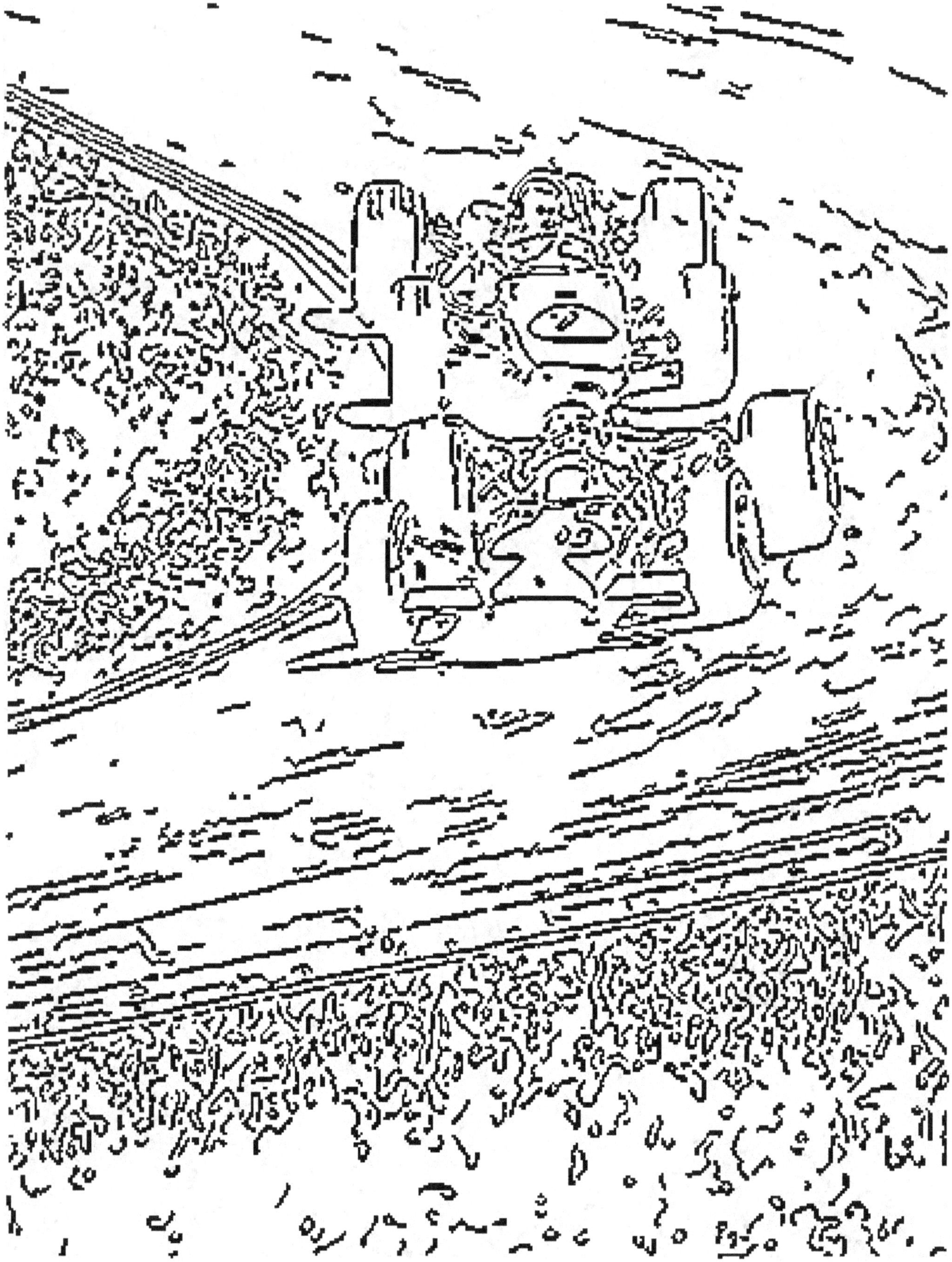

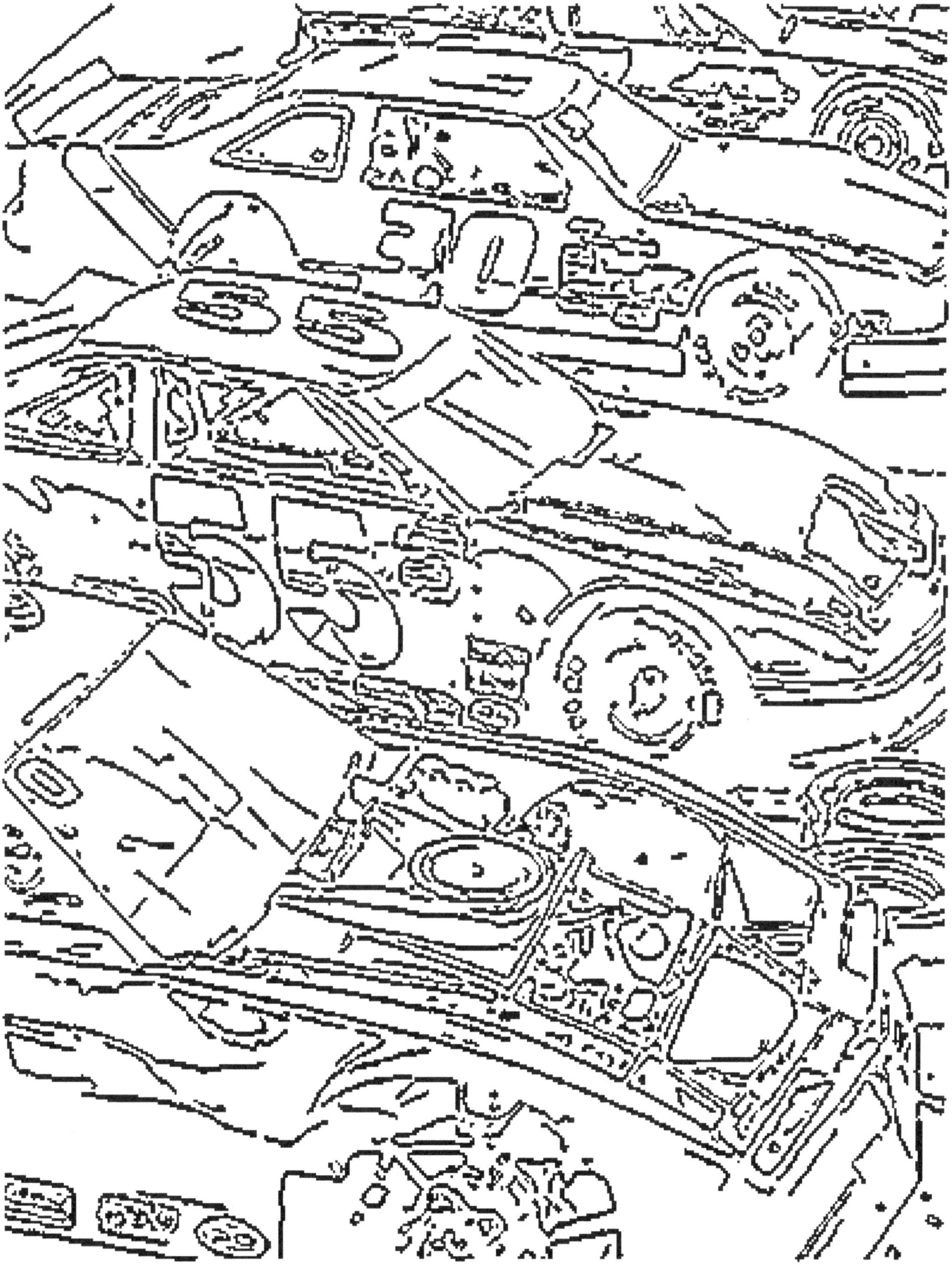

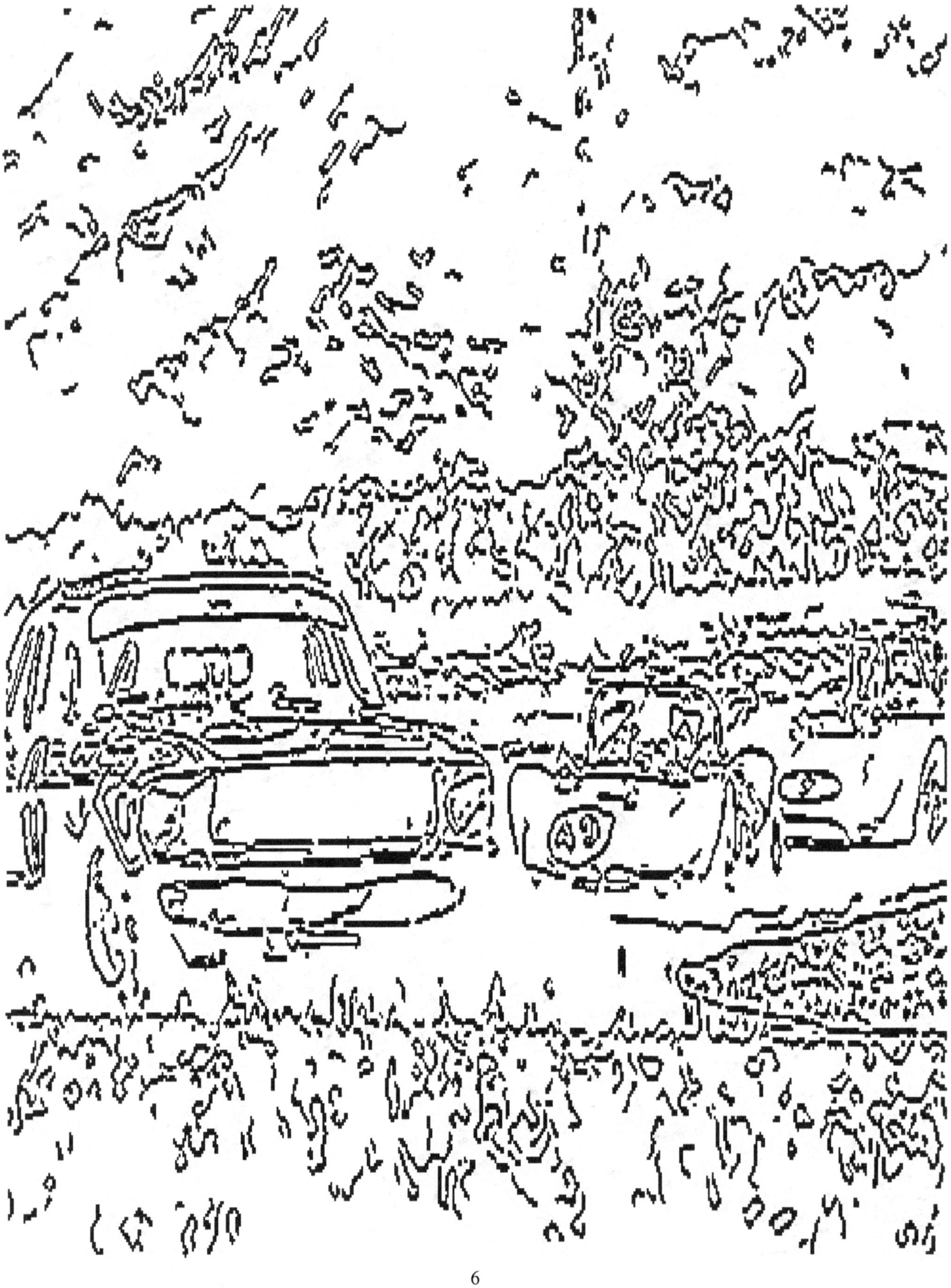

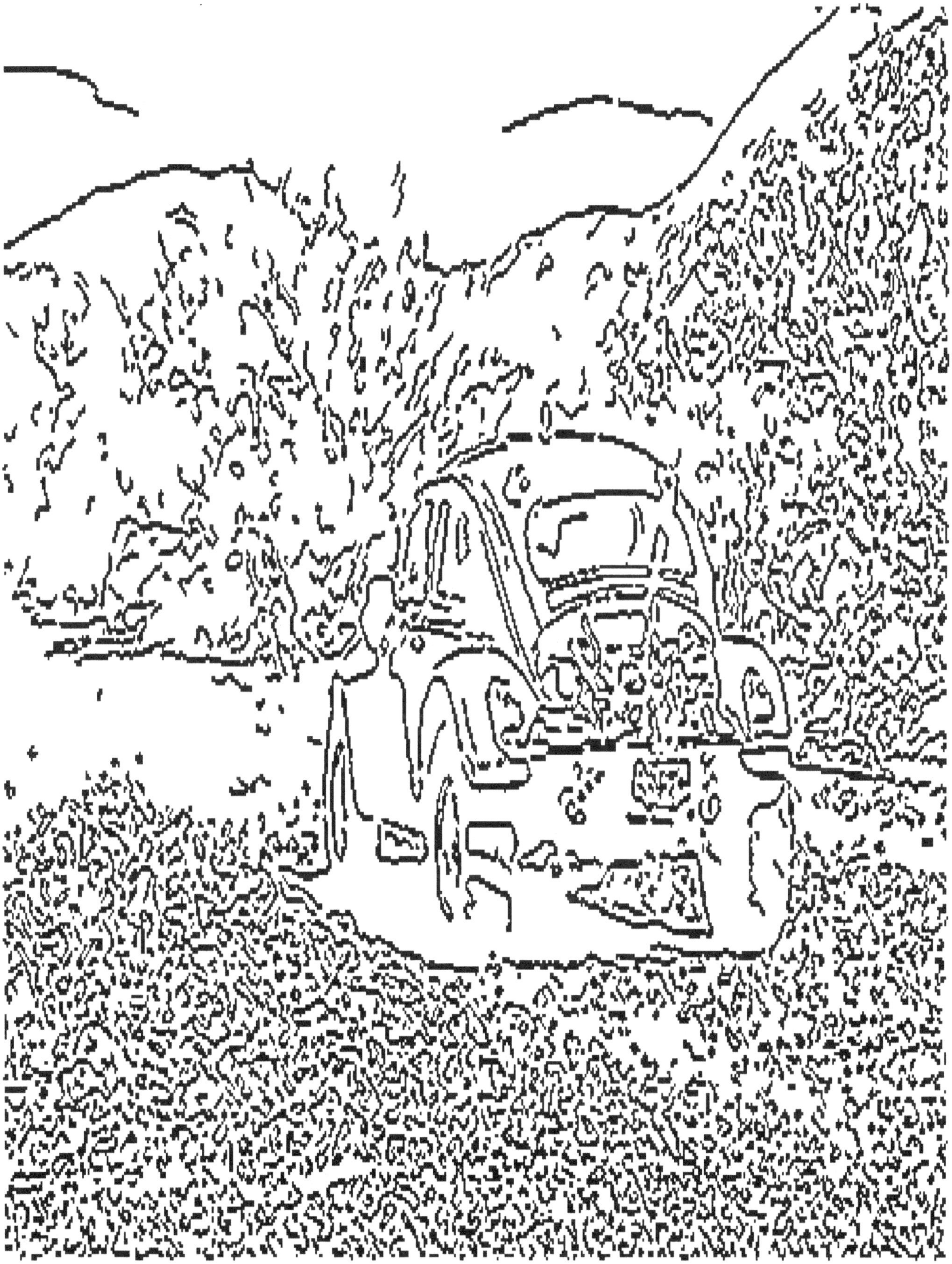

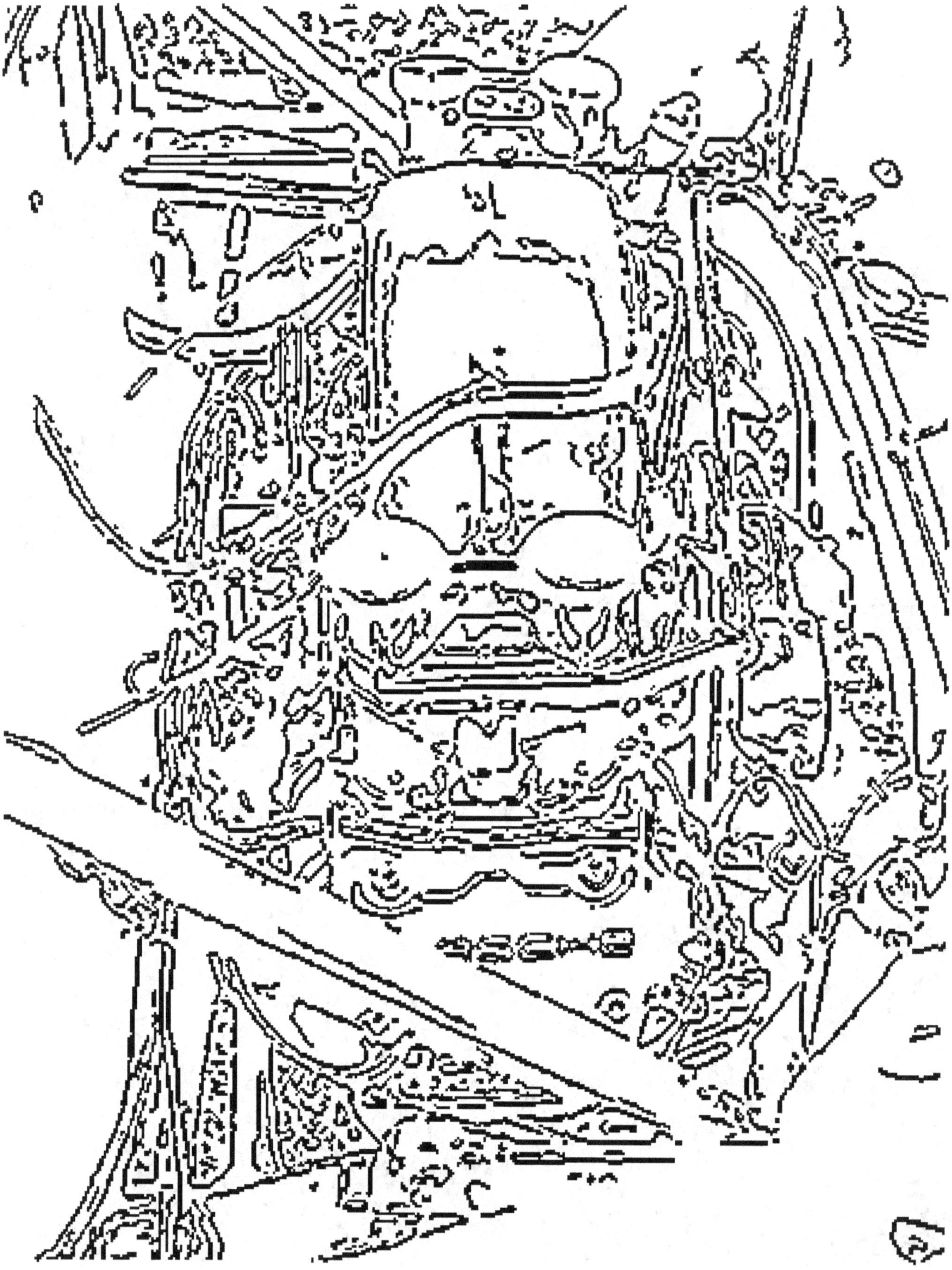

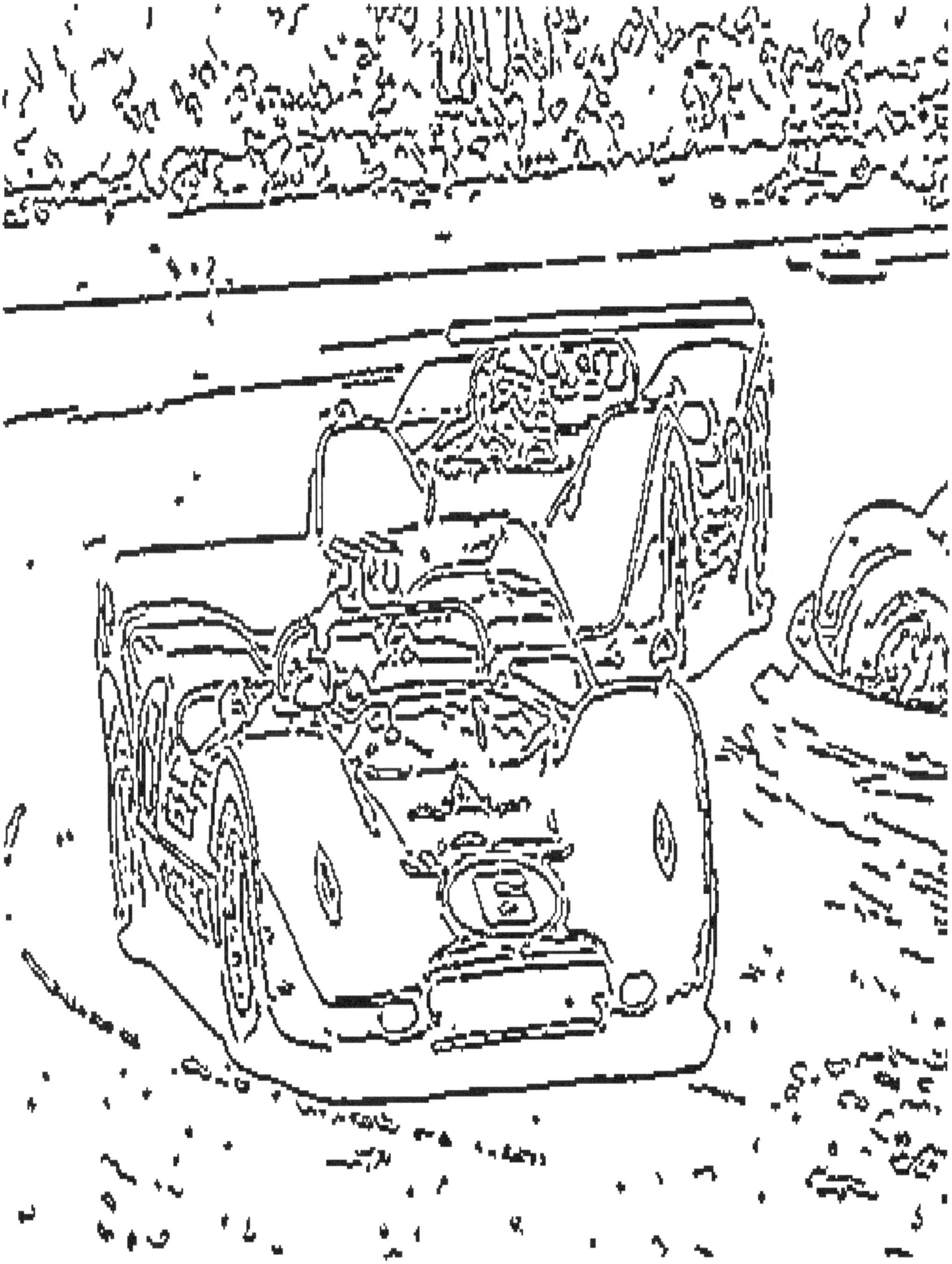

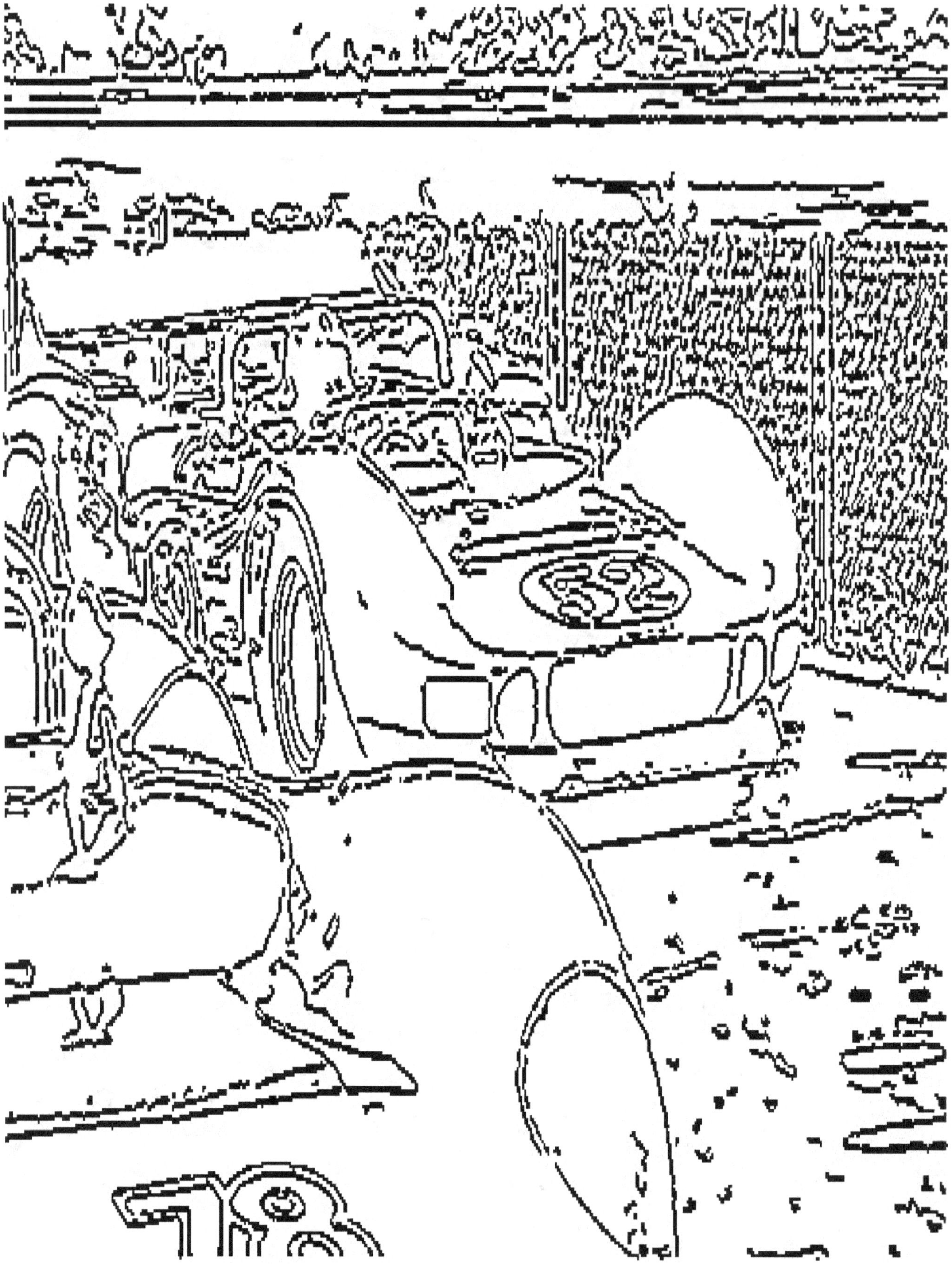
32
18

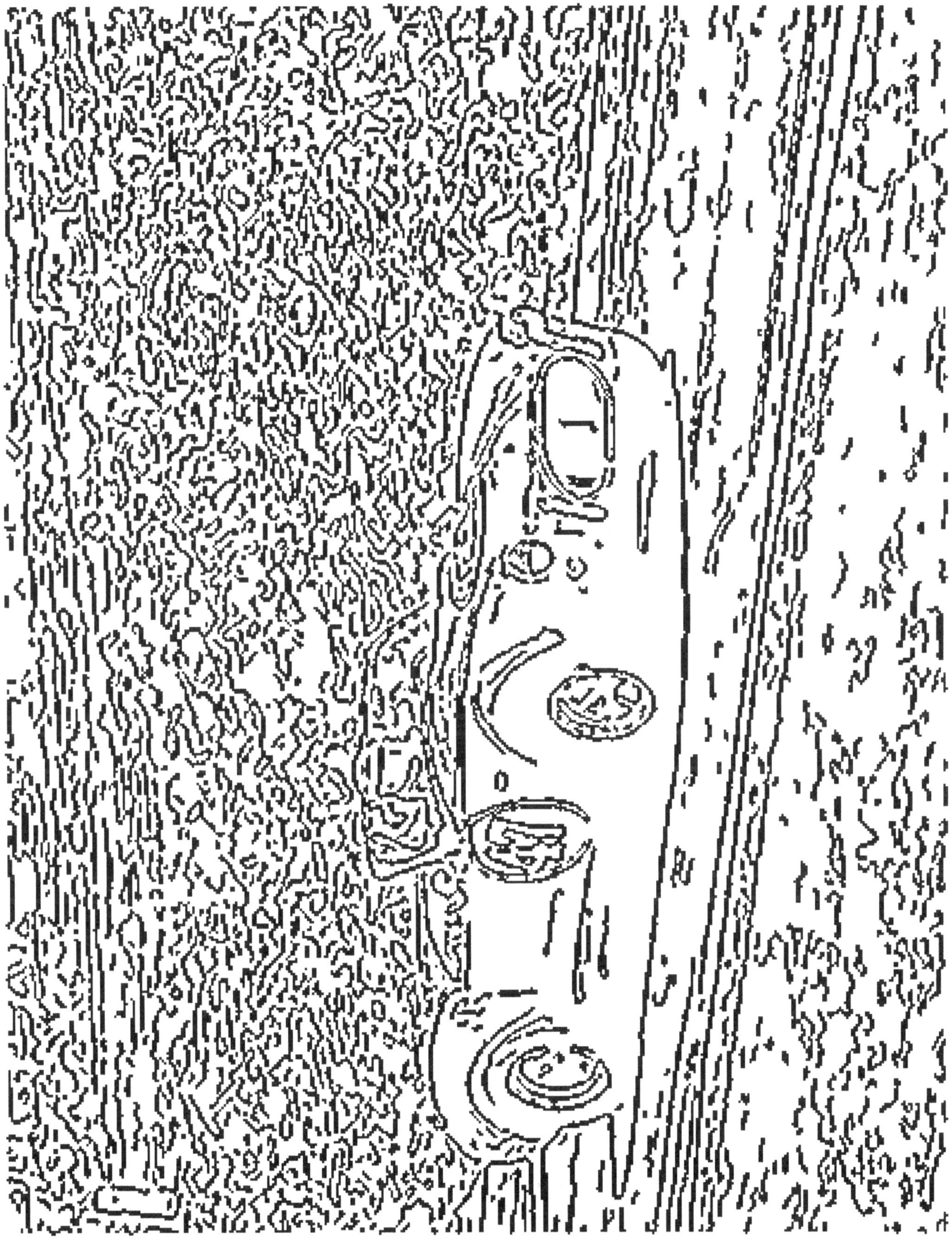

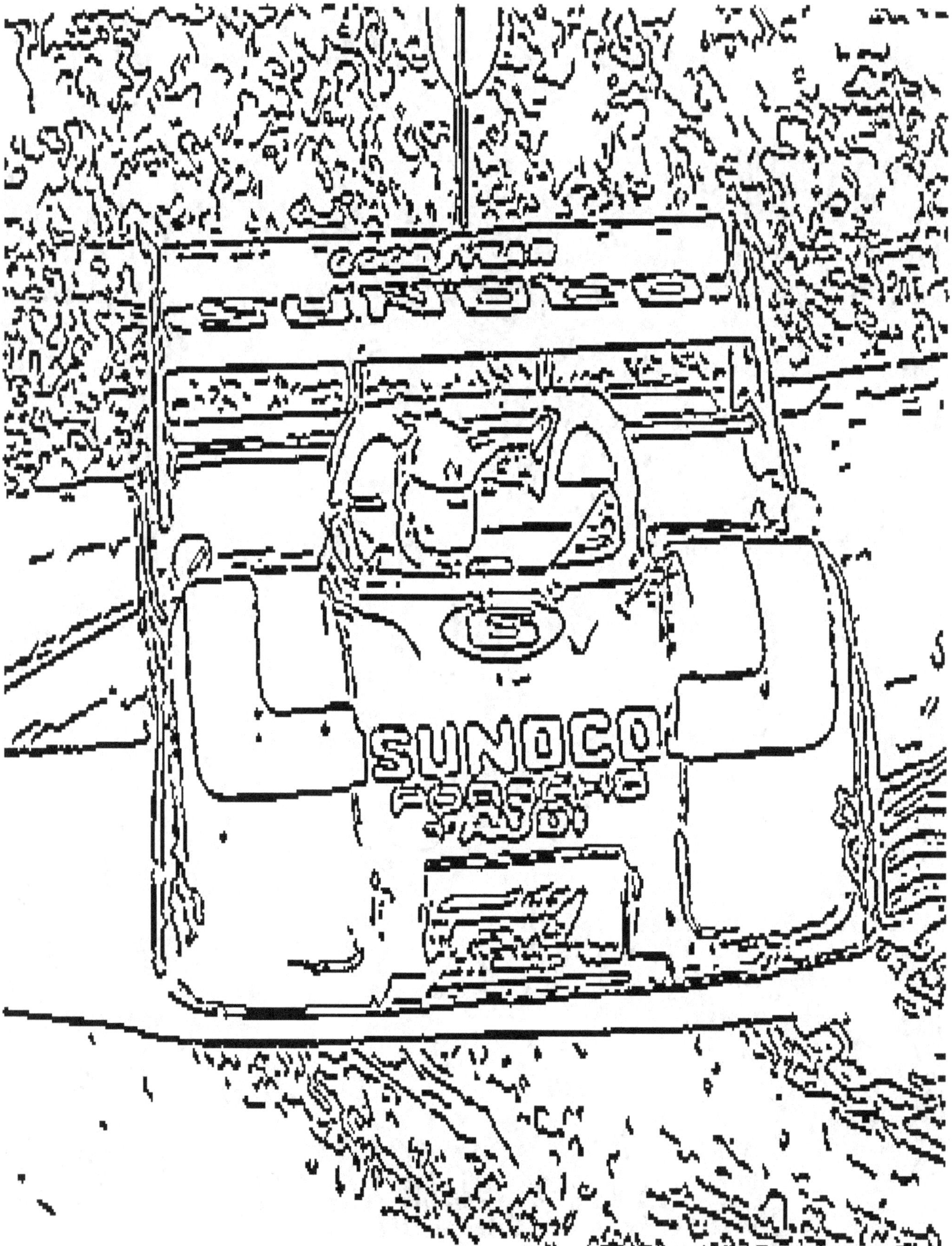
SUNOCO

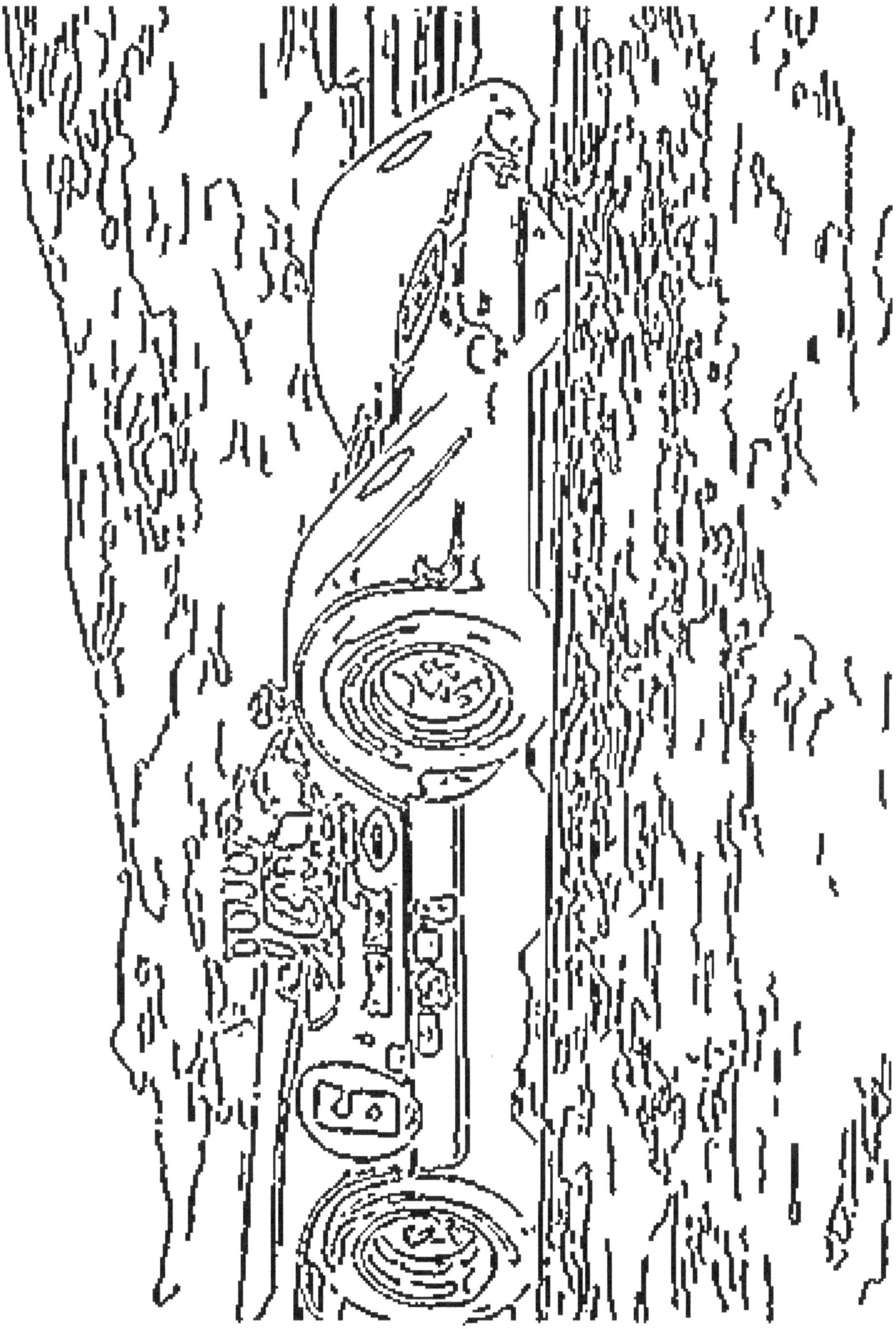

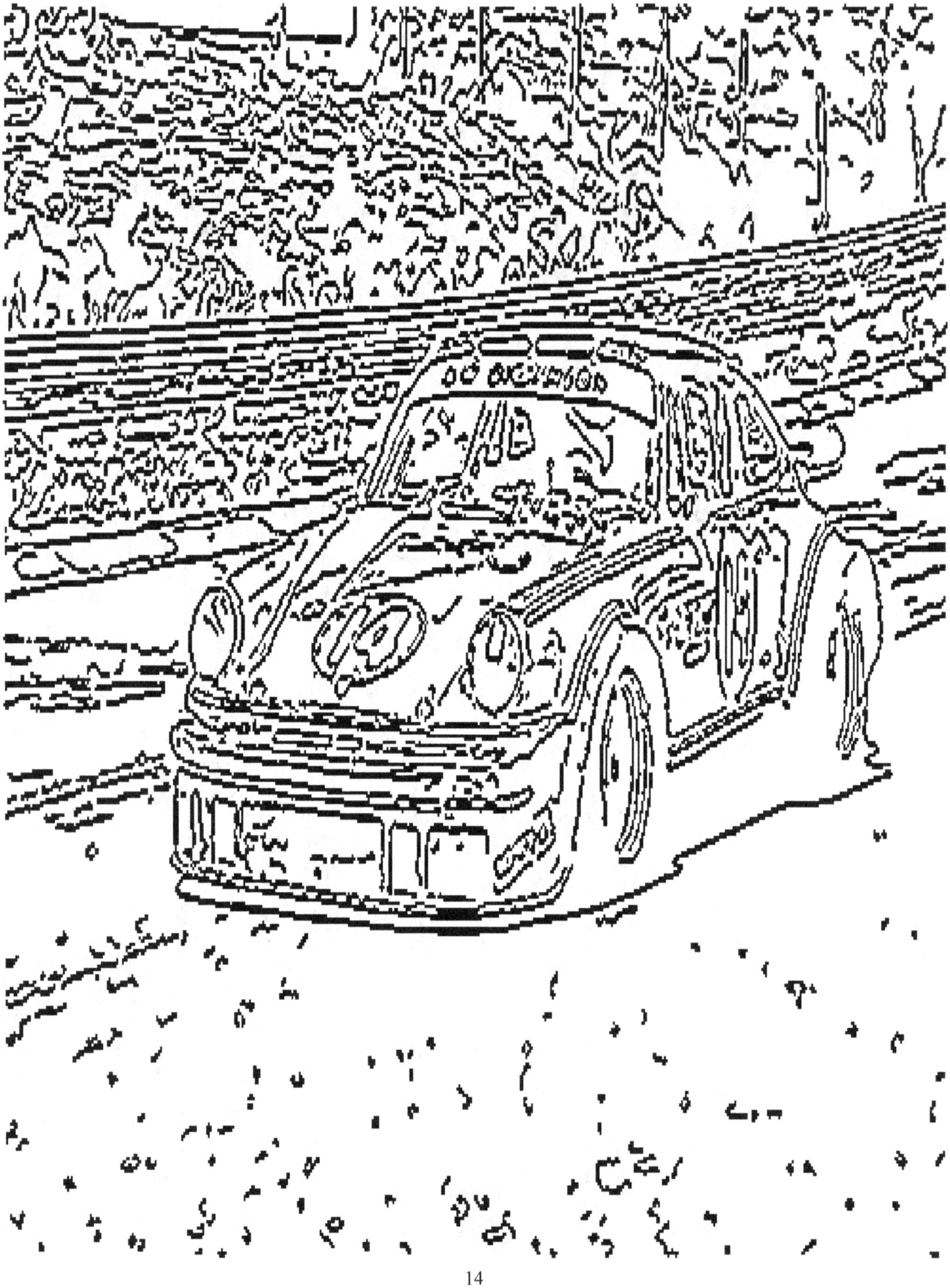

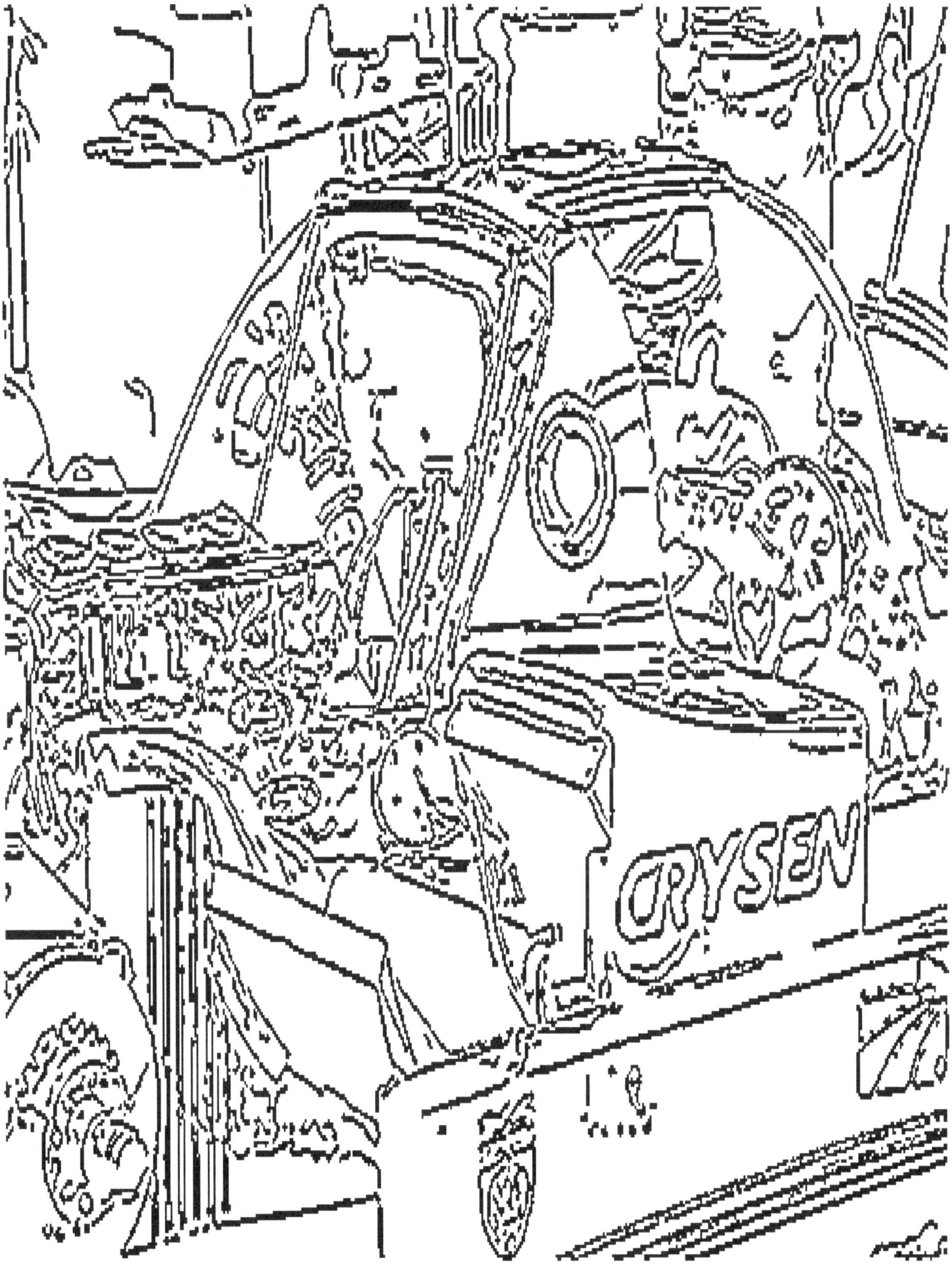
CRYSEN

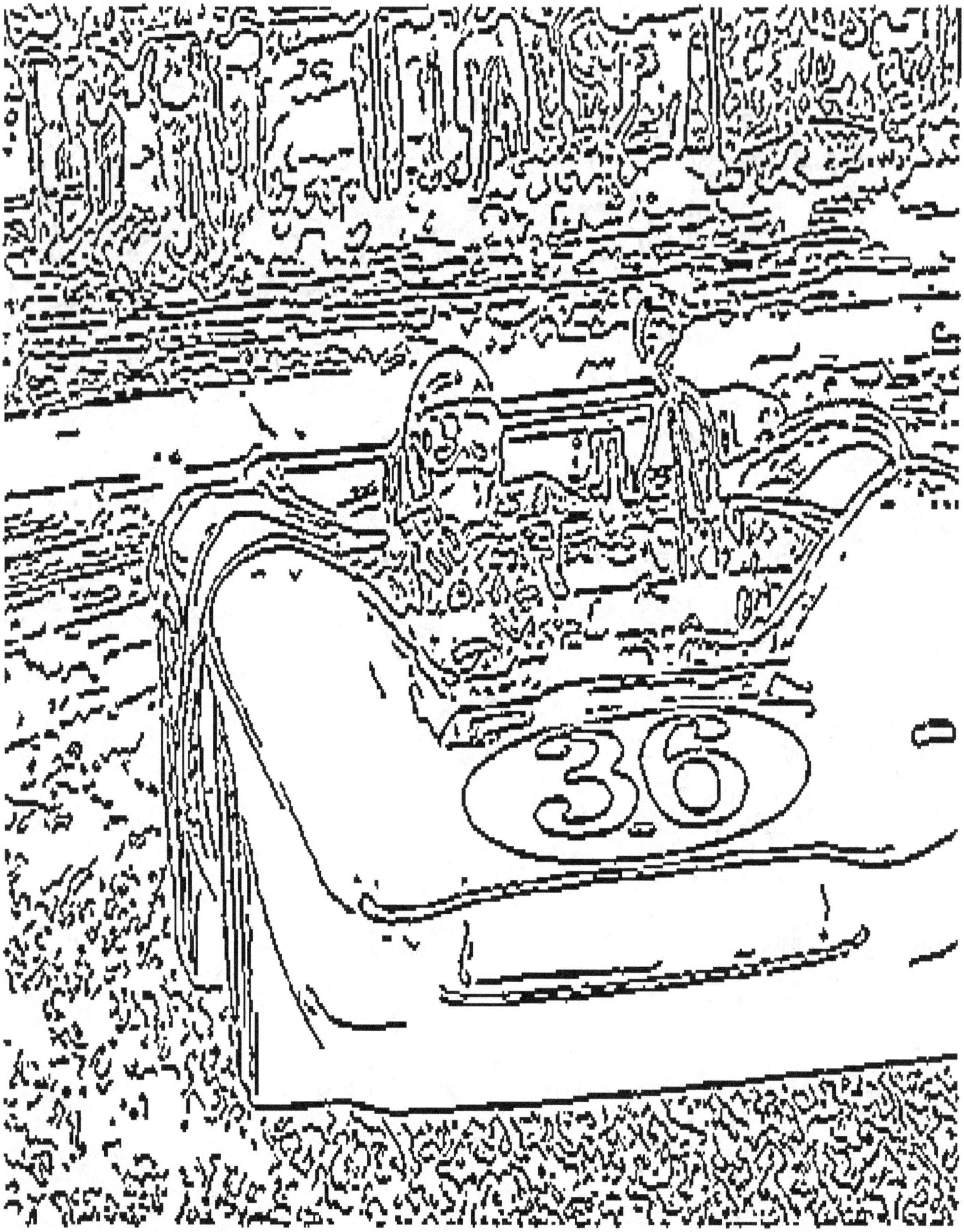
36

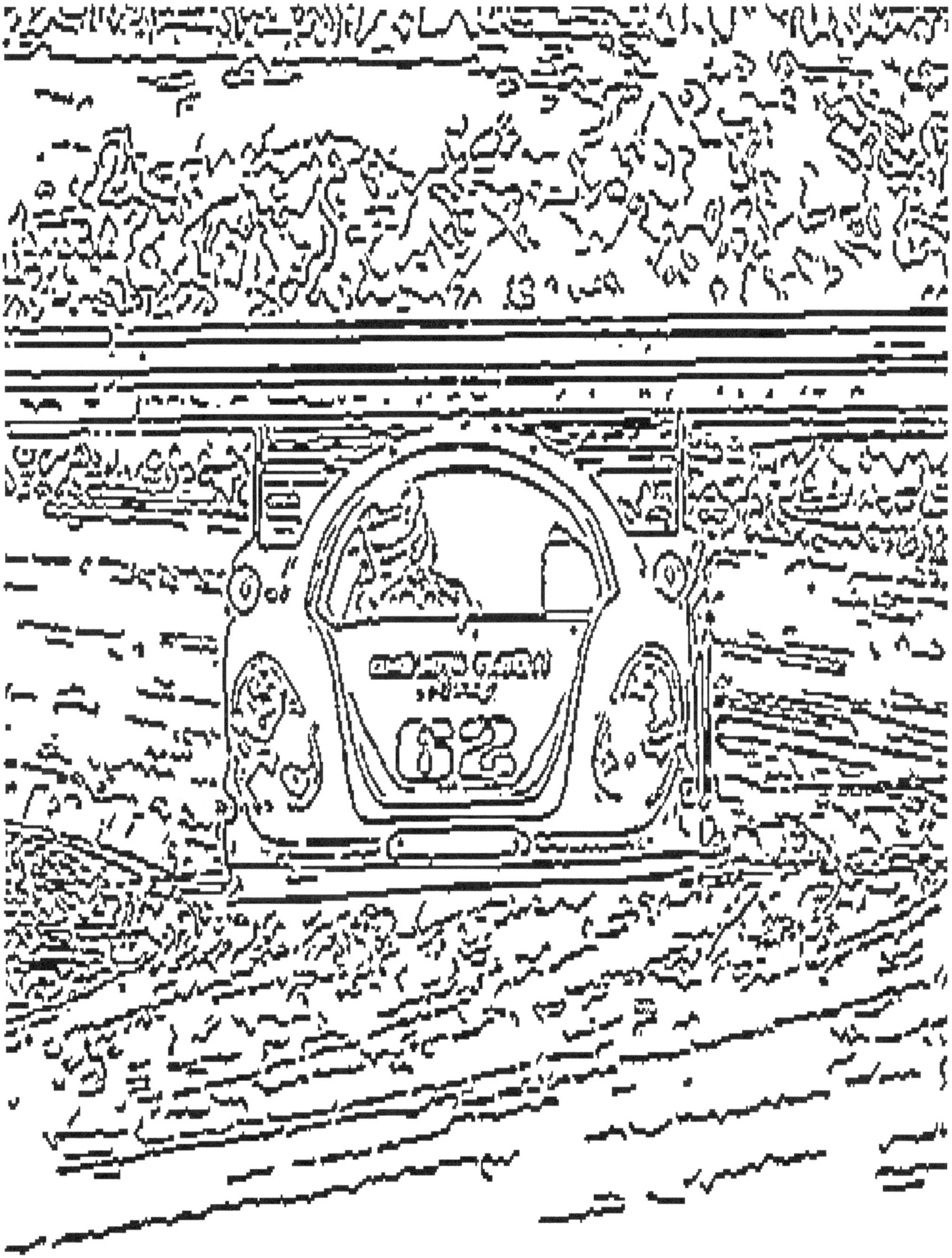

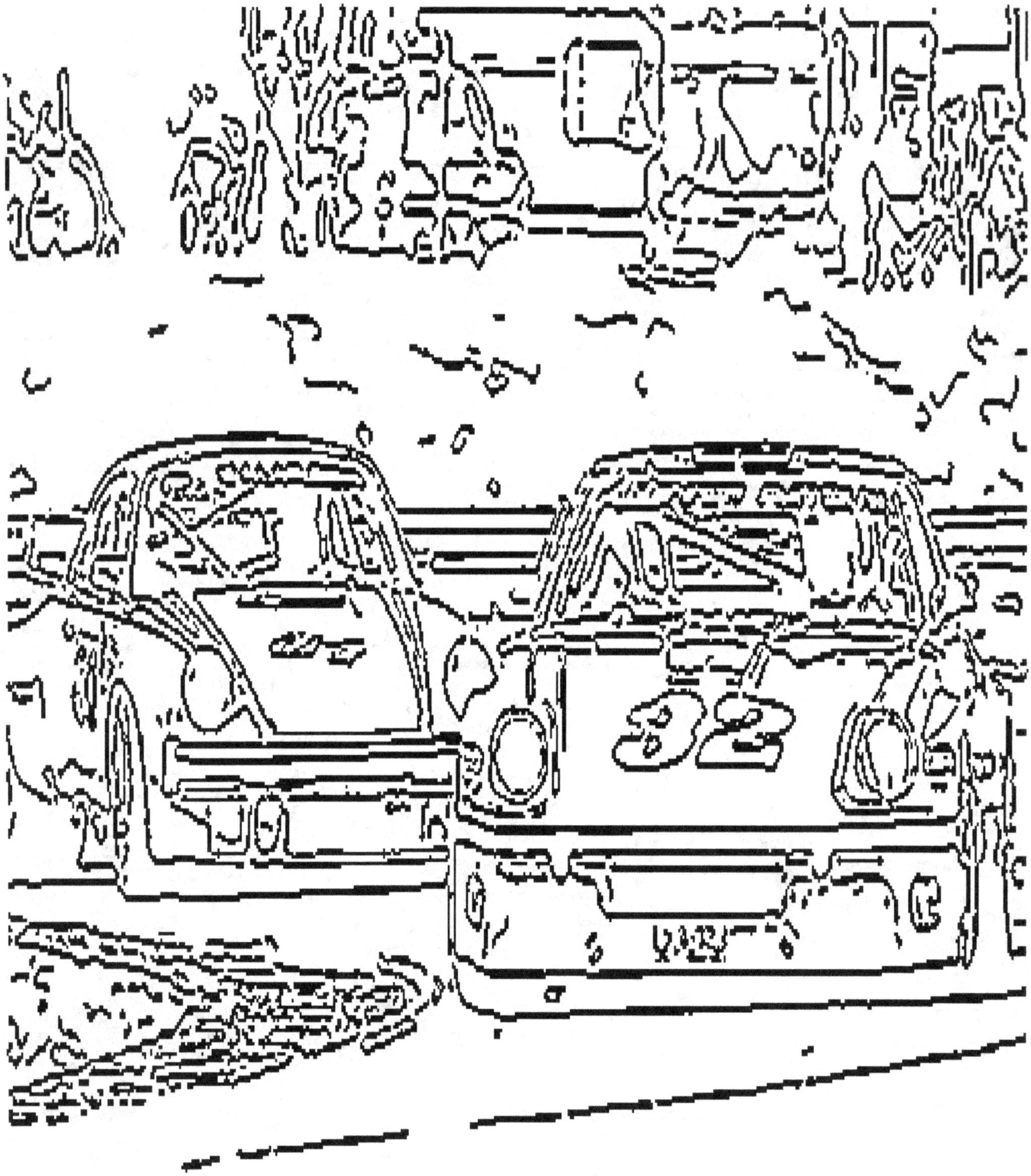
82

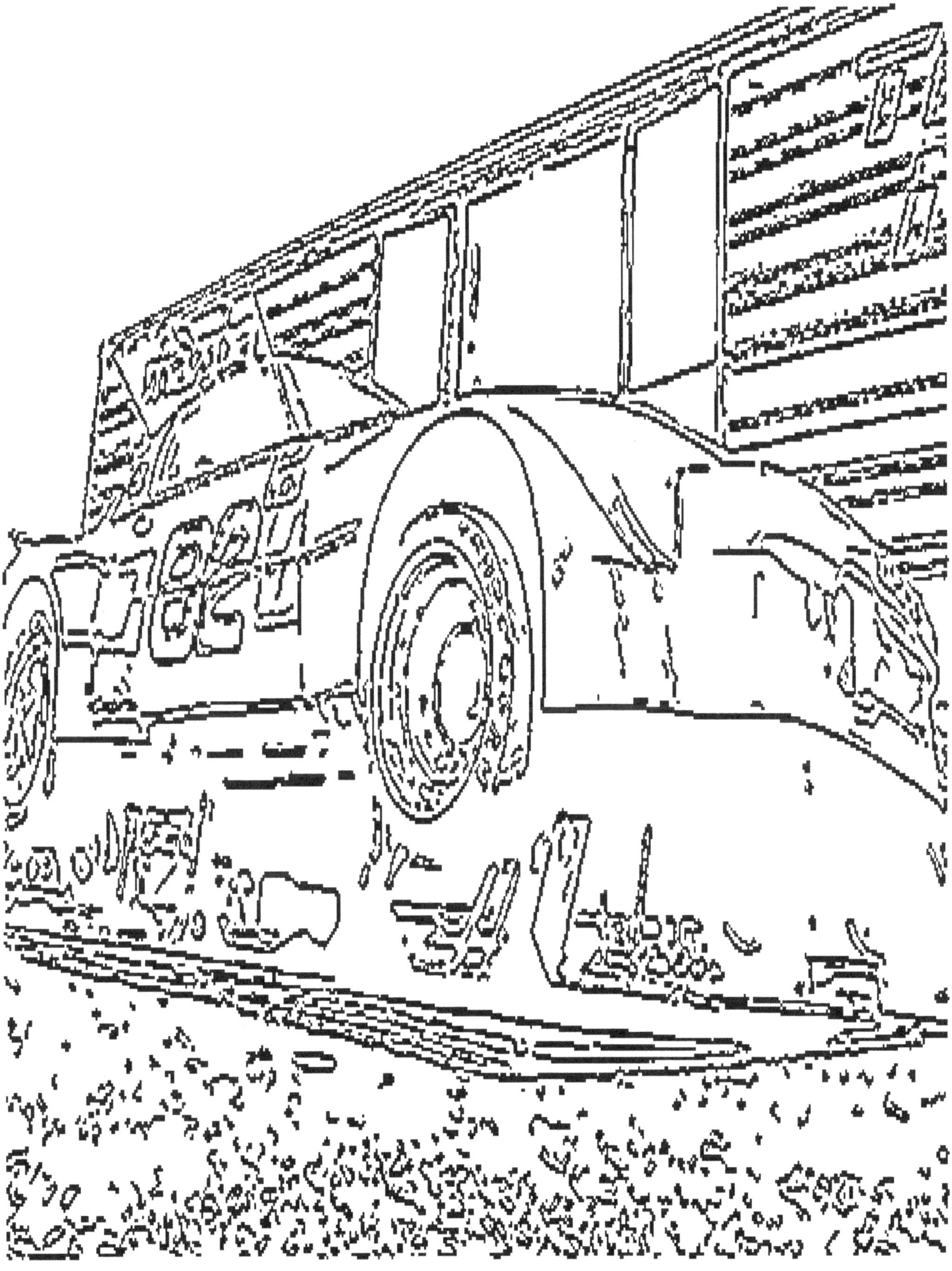

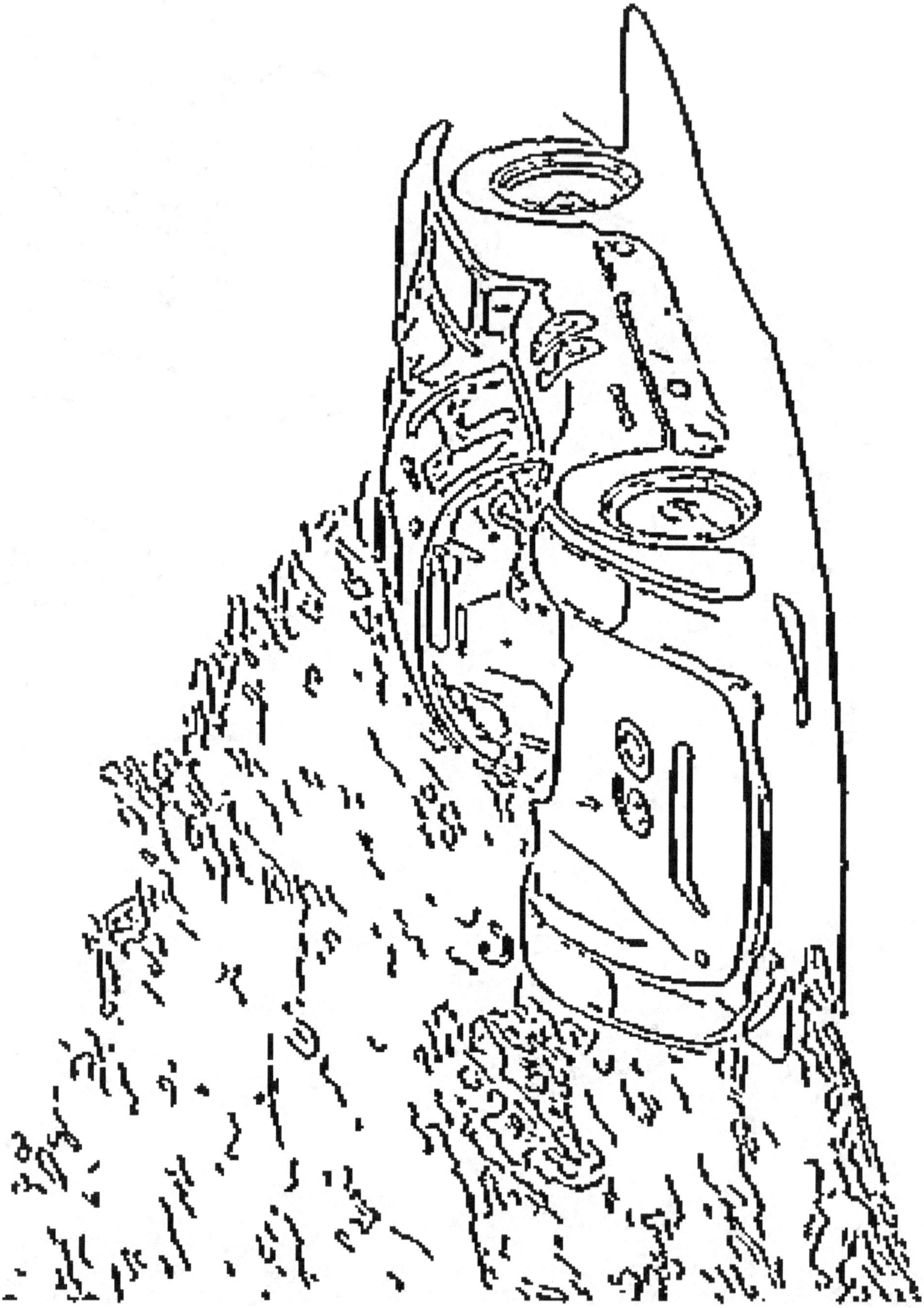

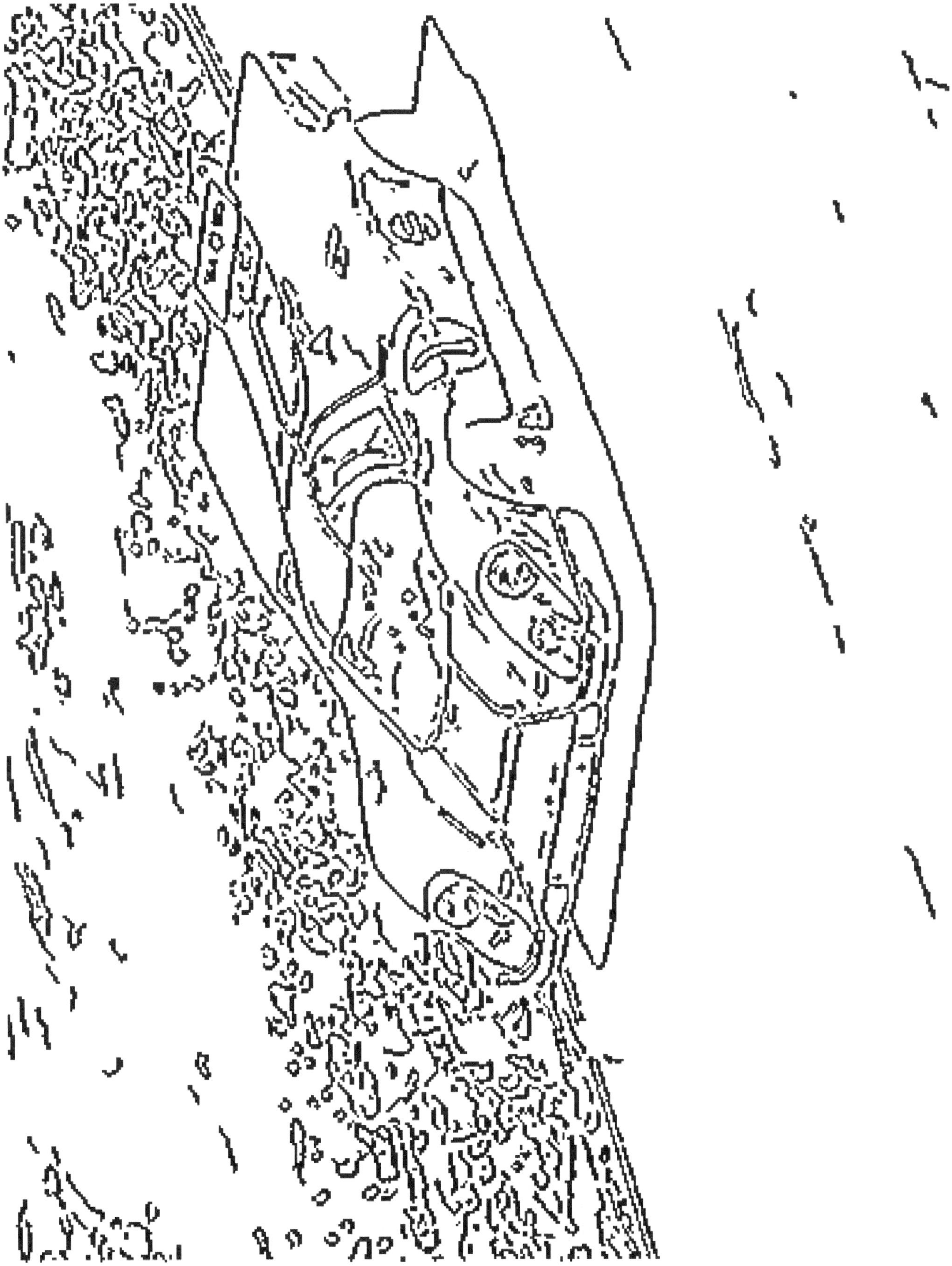

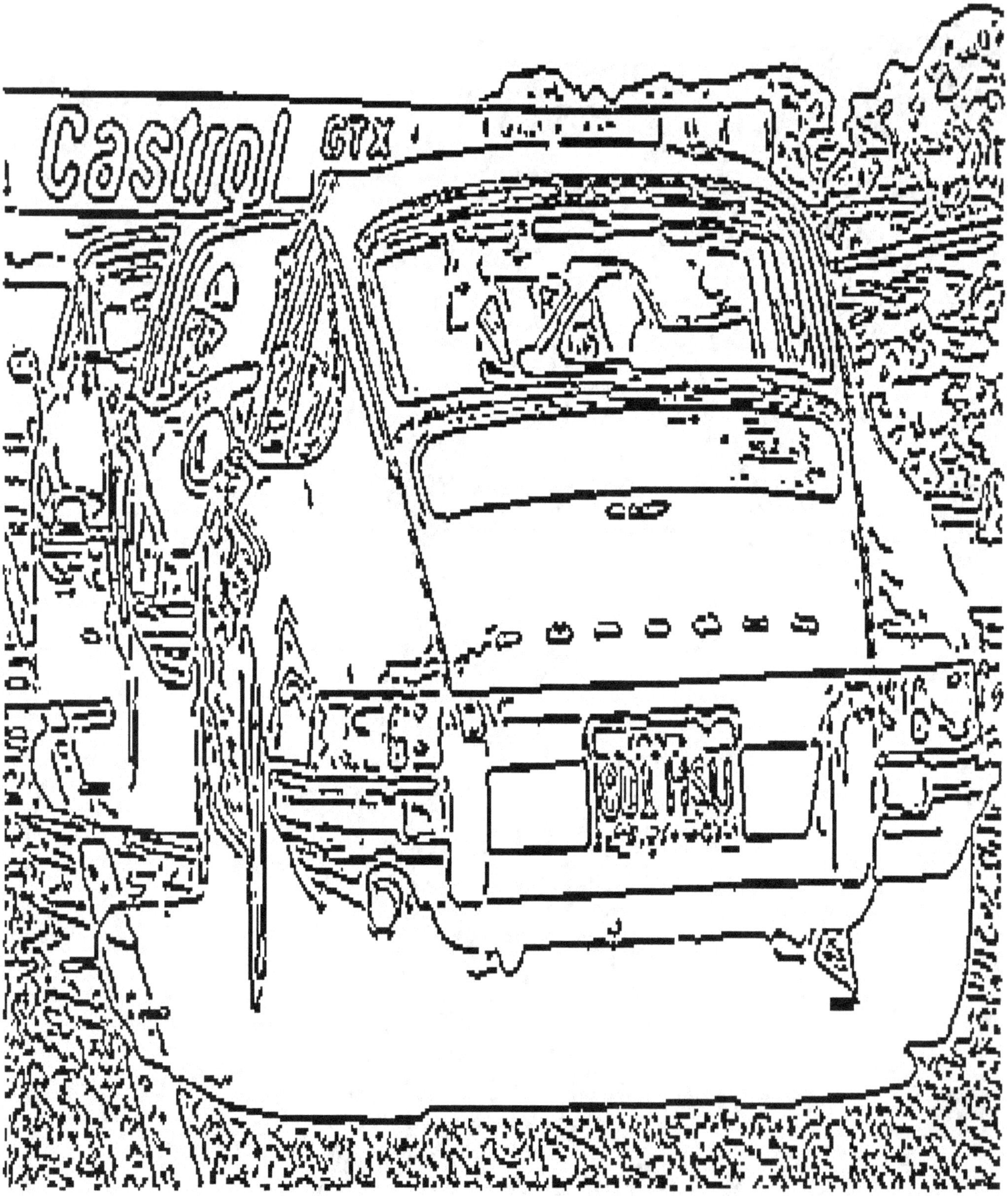
Castrol
GTX

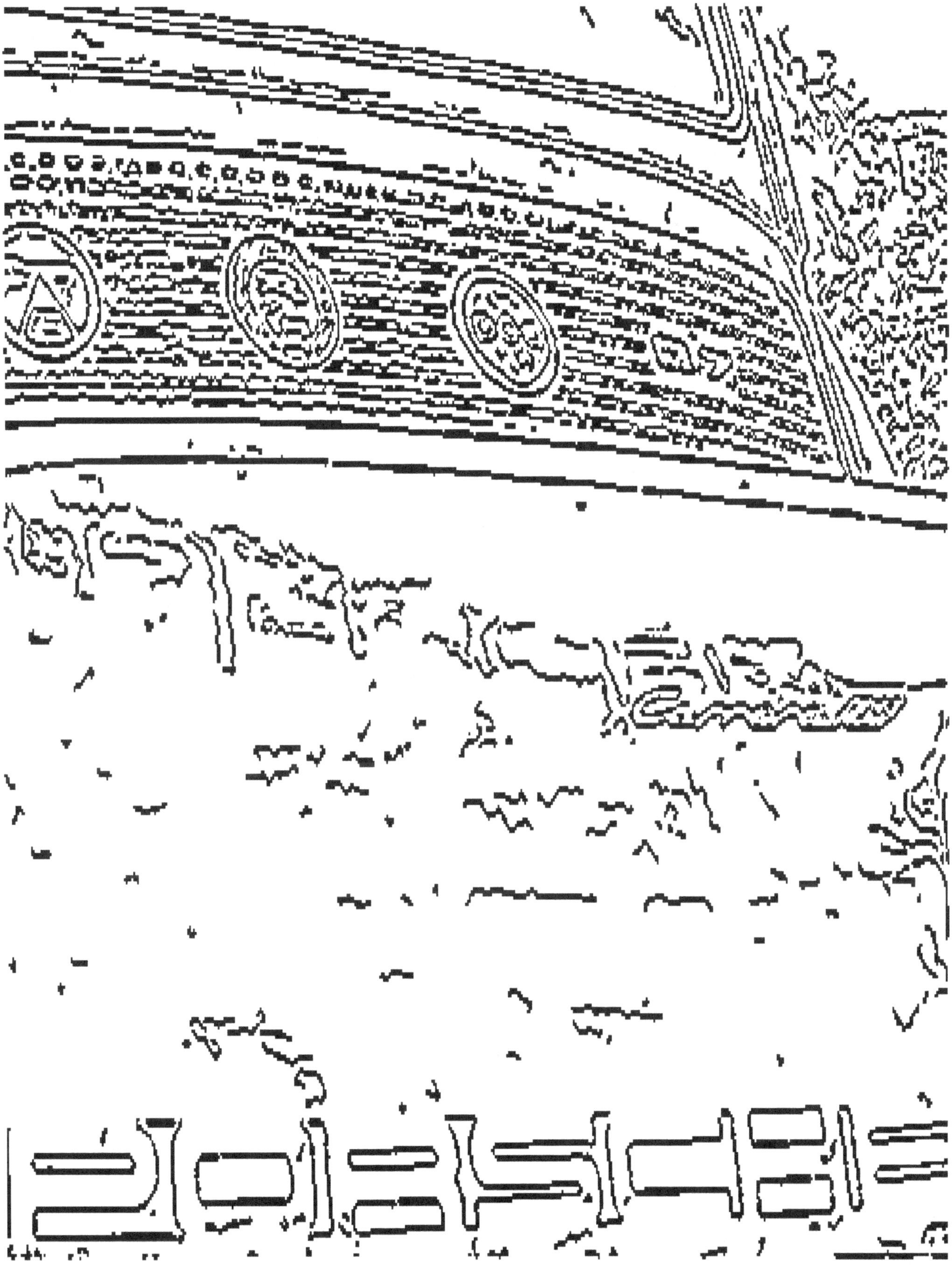

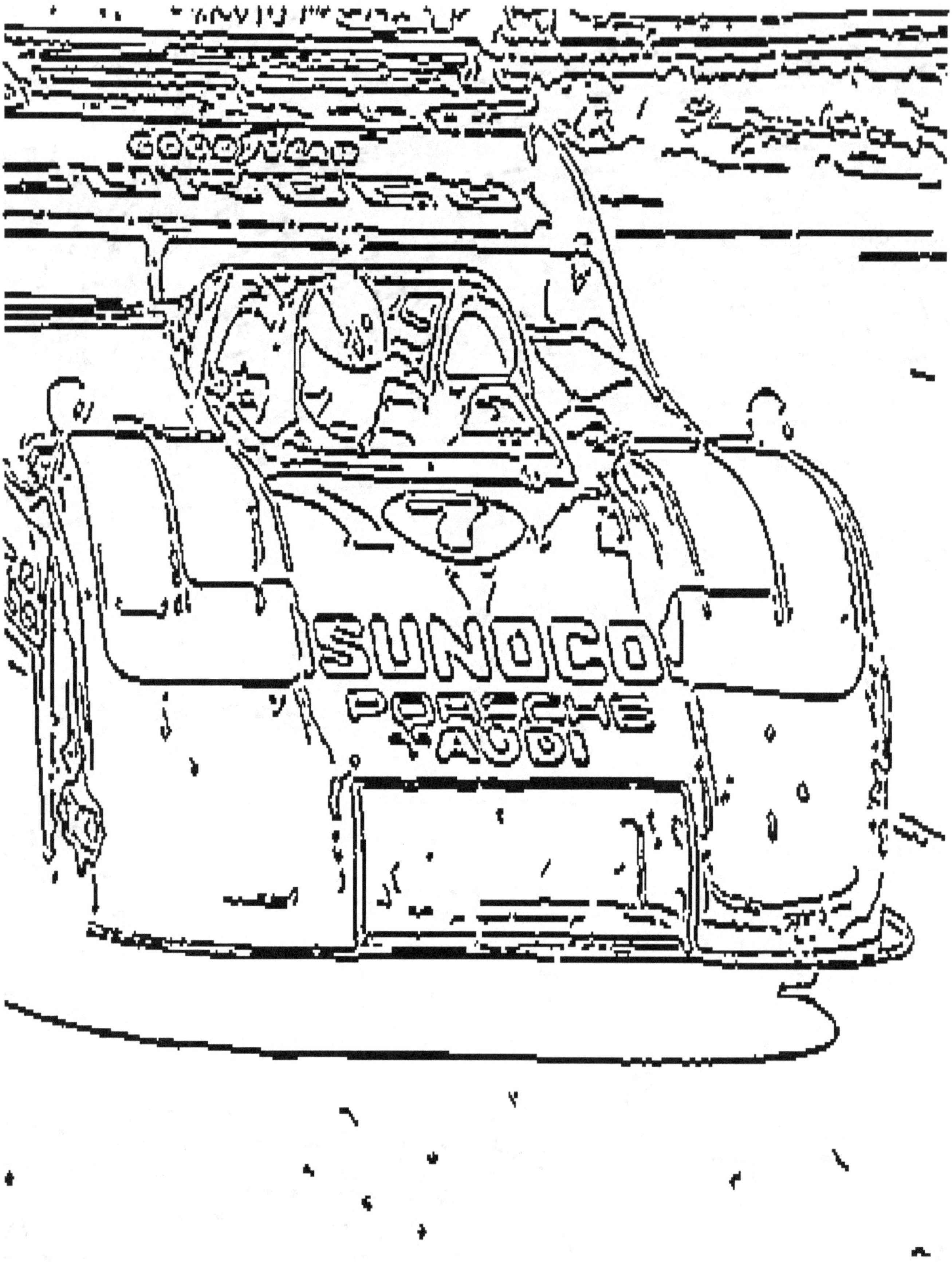
SUNOCO
PORSCHE
AUDI

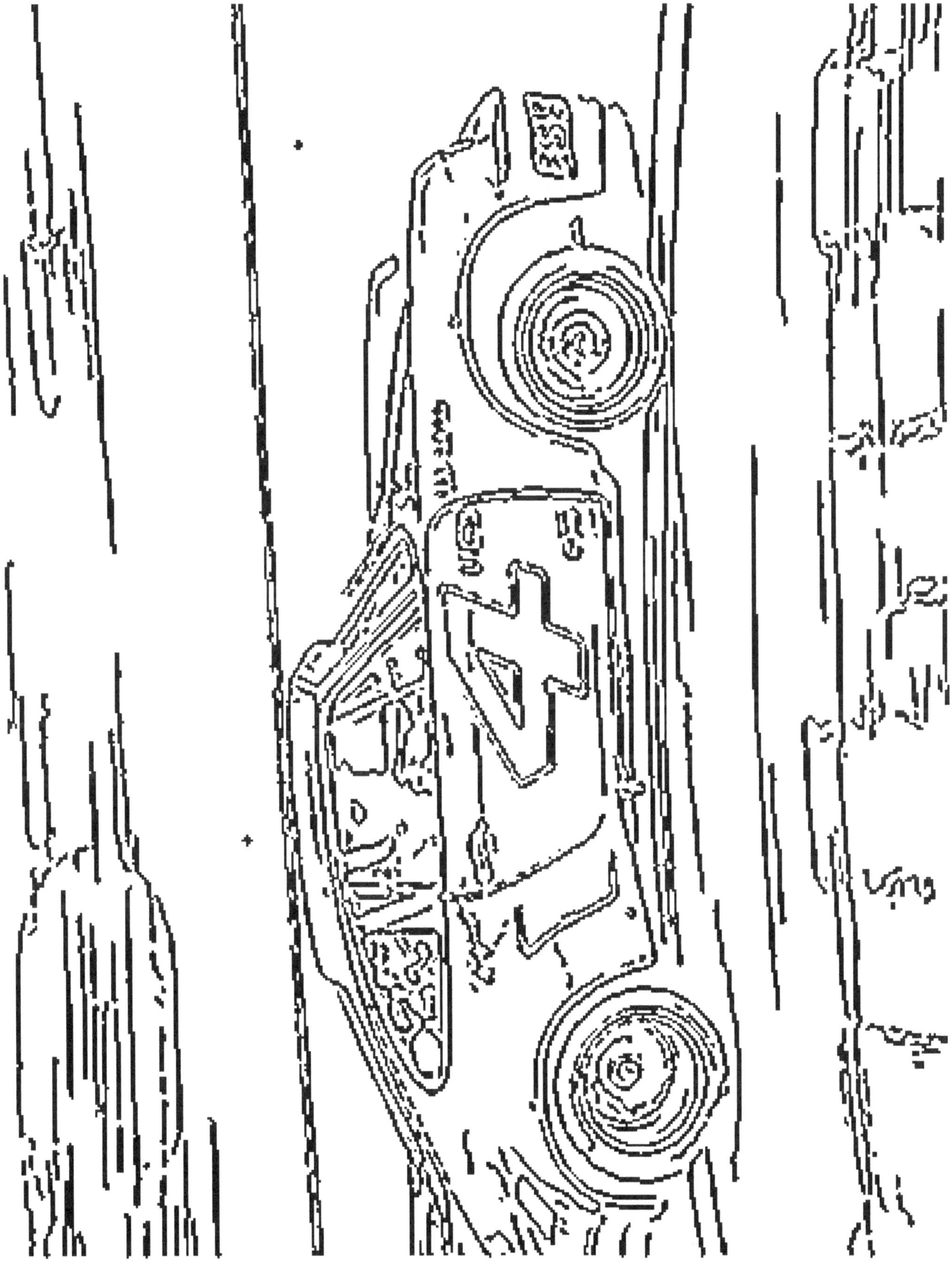

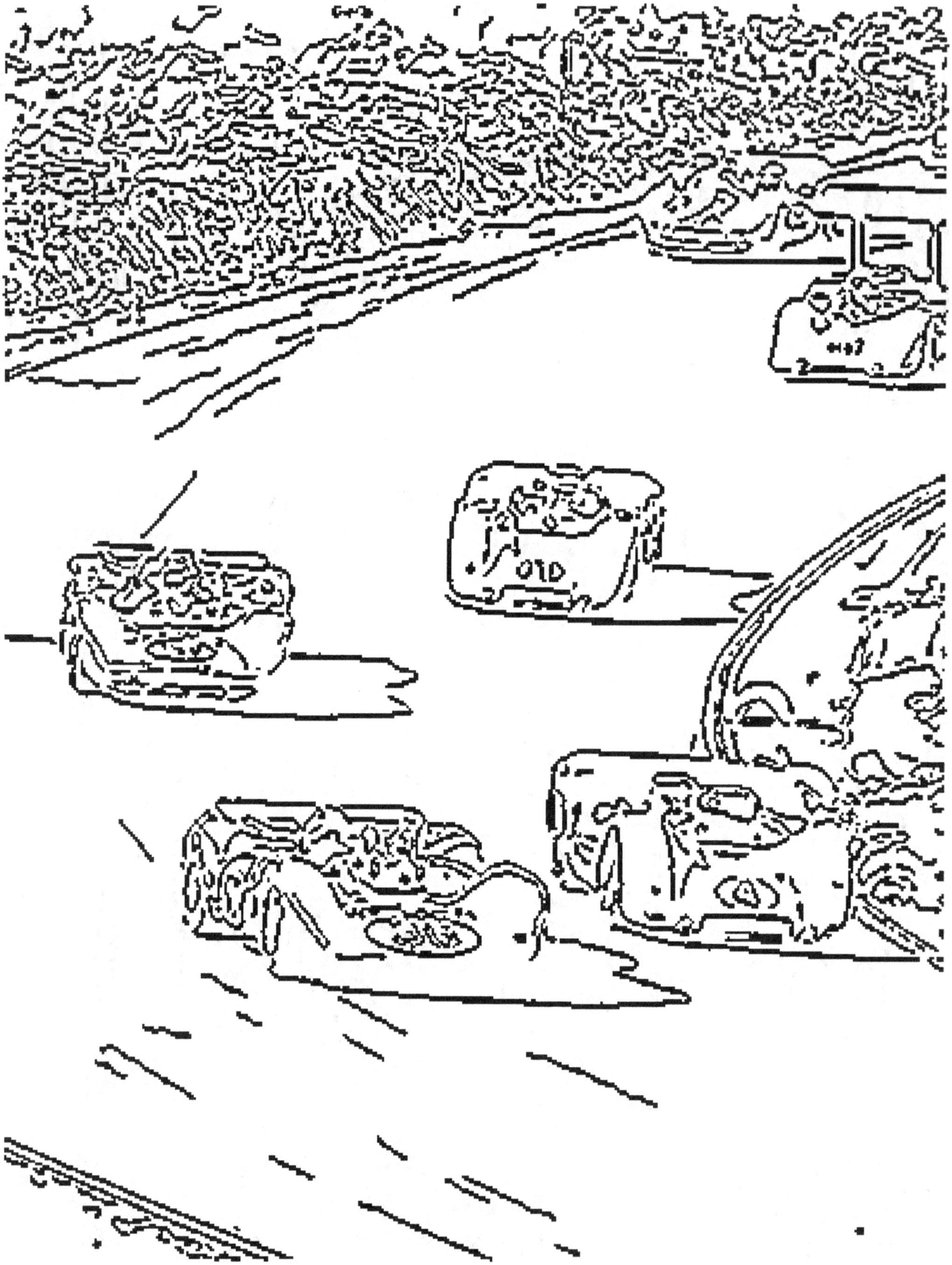

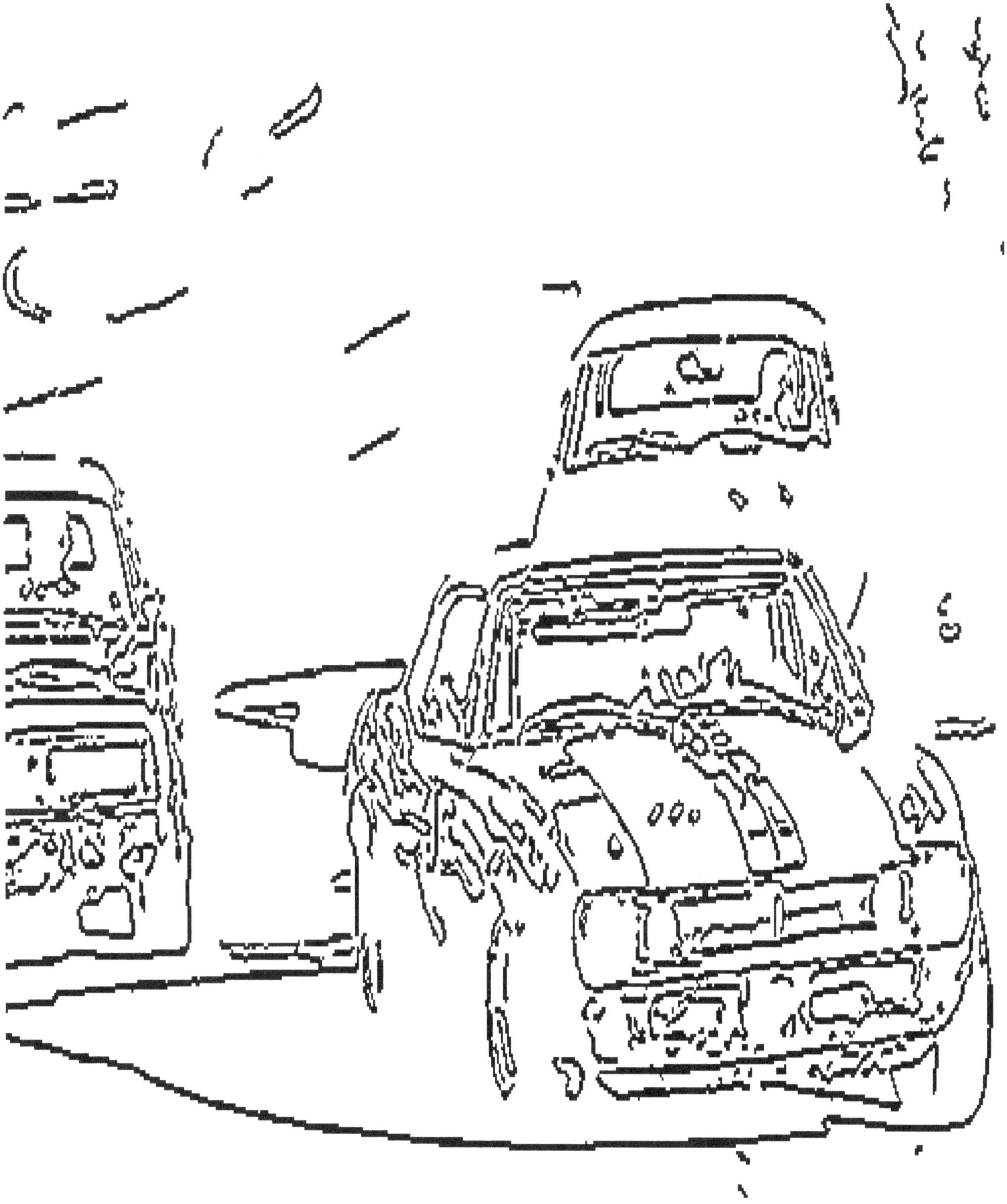

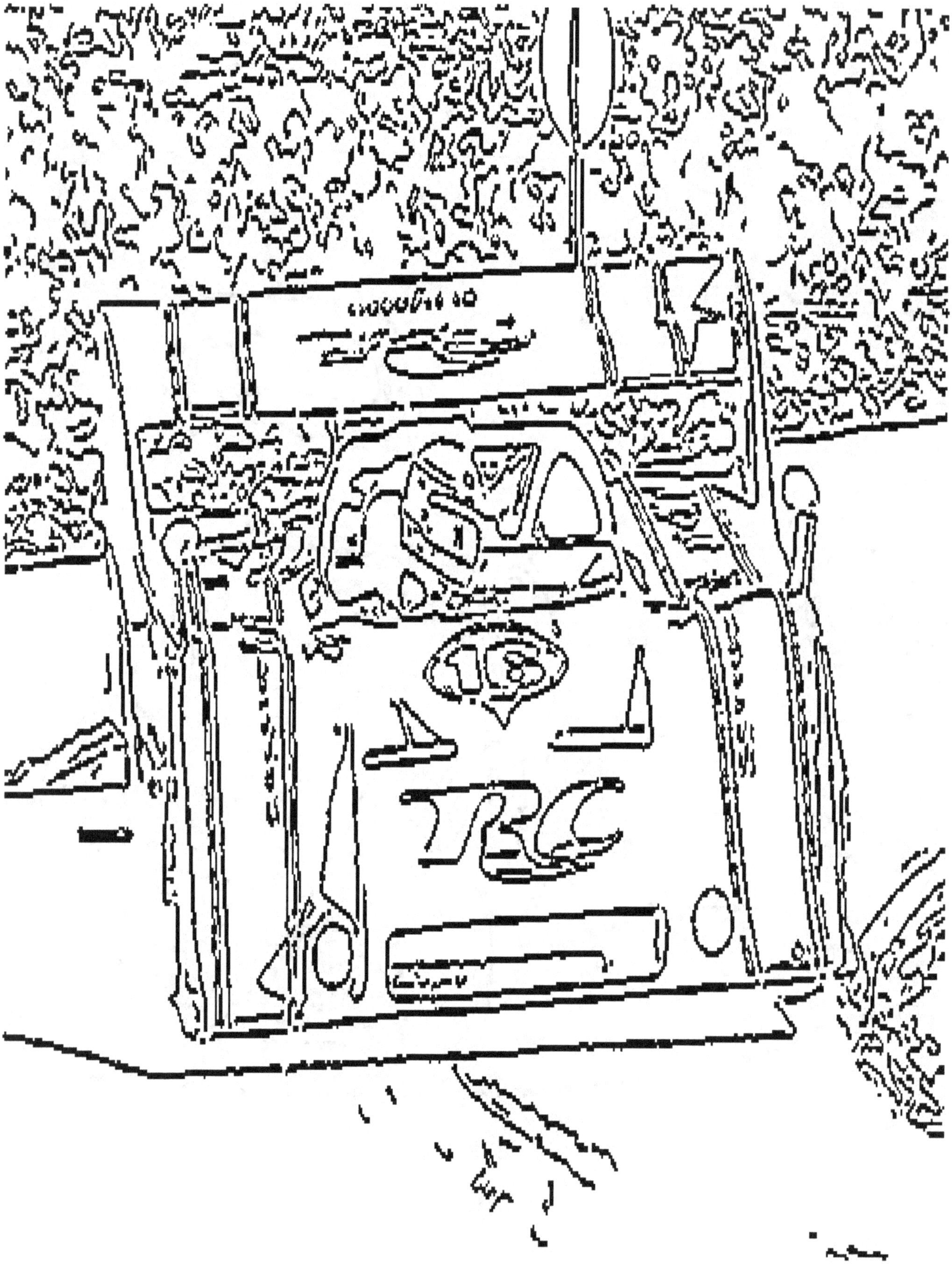
18
TRC

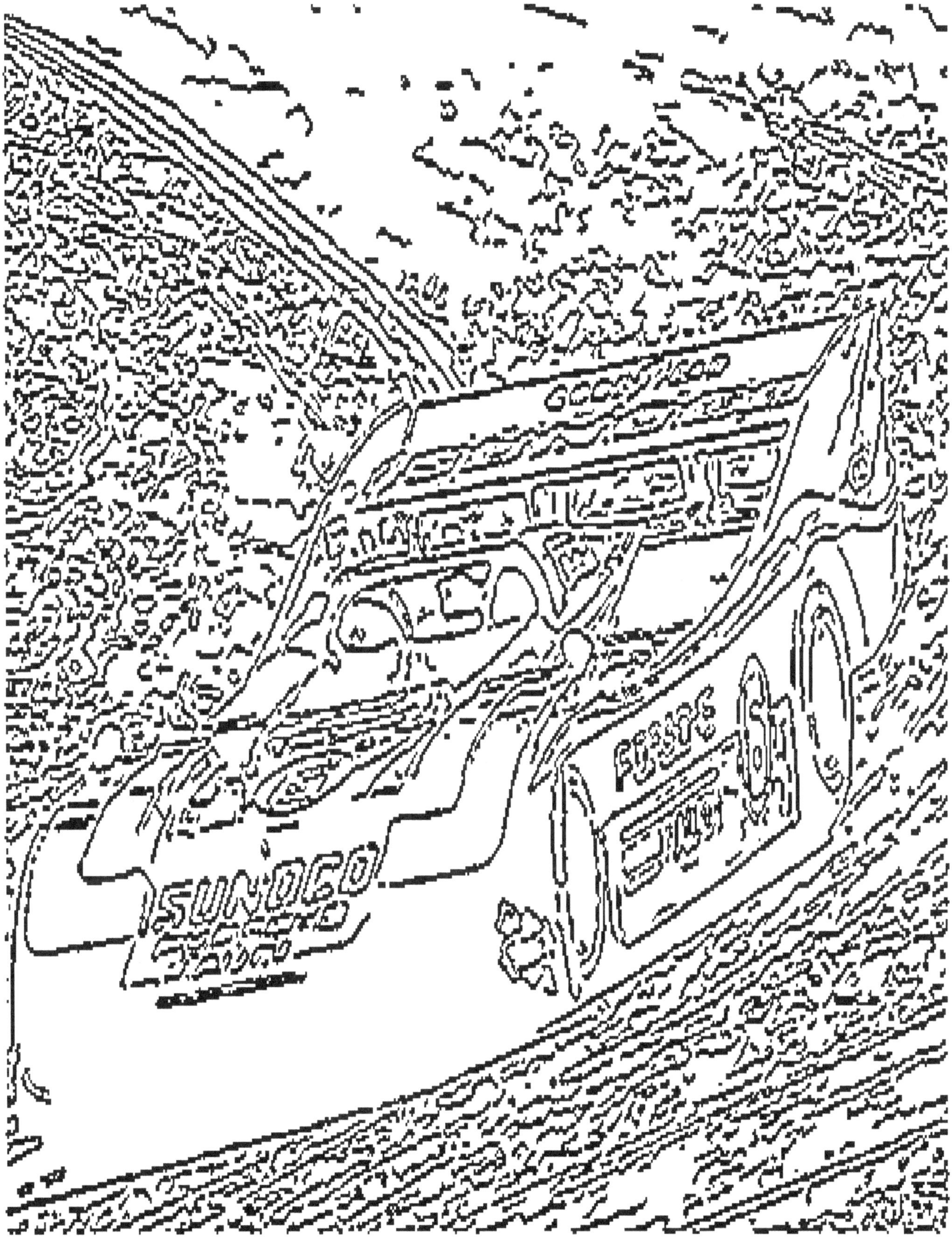
SUNOCO

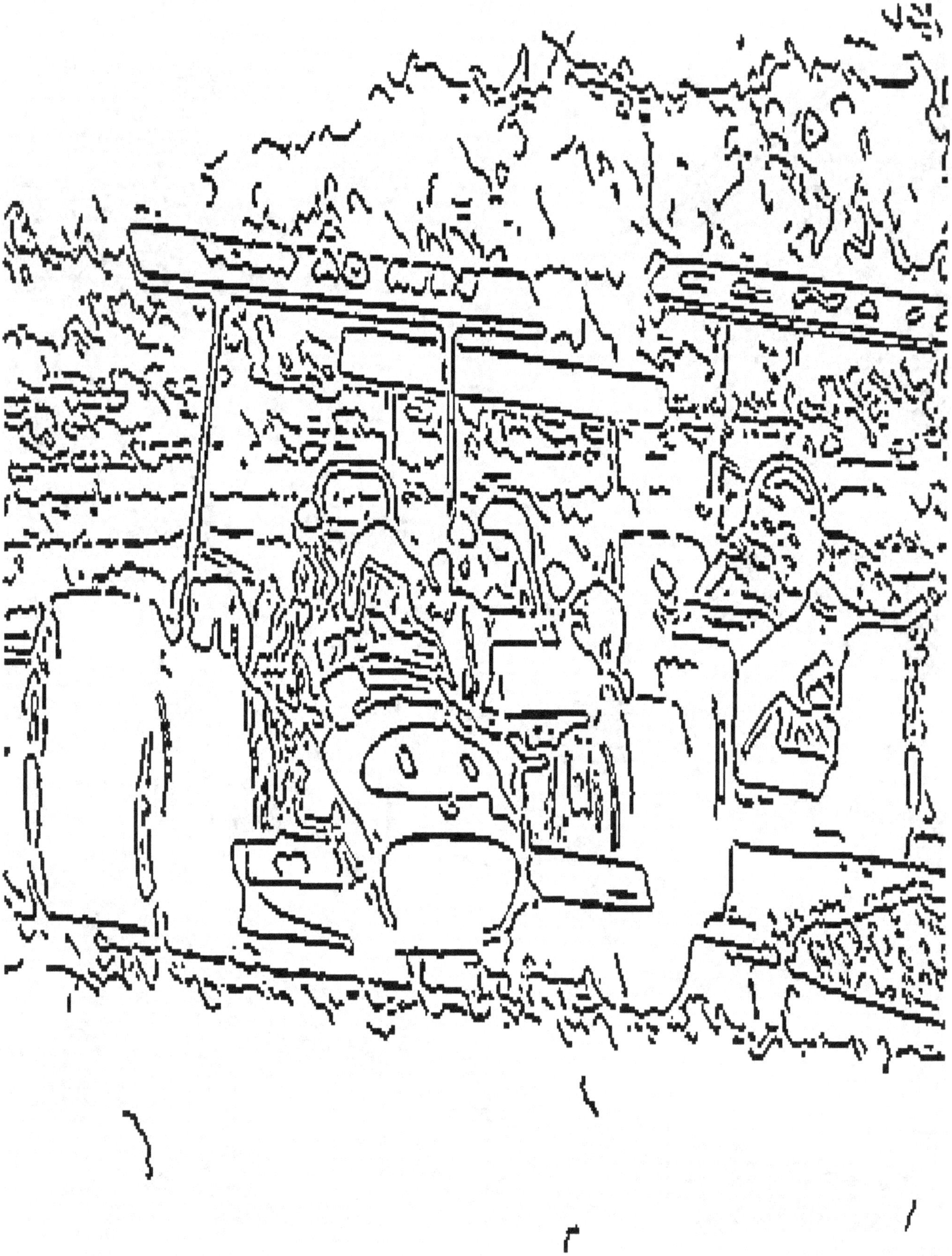

www.ingramcontent.com/pod-product-compliance
Lightning Source LLC
Chambersburg PA
CBHW081315180526
45170CB00007B/2724
* 9 7 8 1 5 4 2 3 8 1 7 9 6 *